麦格希 **中英双语阅读文库**

密探神马

【美】比林斯 (Billings, H.)　【美】比林斯 (Billings, M.) ●主编

杨恒●译

麦格希中英双语阅读文库编委会●编

 全国百佳图书出版单位

吉林出版集团股份有限公司

图书在版编目（CIP）数据

密探神马 / (美) 比林斯 (Billings. H) , (美) 比
林斯 (Billings. M) 主编 ; 麦格希中英双语阅读文
库编委会编 ; 杨恒译. -- 2版. -- 长春 : 吉林出
版集团股份有限公司, 2018.3（2022.1重印）
（麦格希中英双语阅读文库）
ISBN 978-7-5581-4731-9

Ⅰ.①密… Ⅱ.①比… ②比… ③麦… ④杨… Ⅲ.
①英语—汉语—对照读物 Ⅳ.①H319.4

中国版本图书馆CIP数据核字(2018)第045919号

密探神马

编：	麦格希中英双语阅读文库编委会	
插　画：	齐　航　李延霞	
责任编辑：	沈丽娟	
封面设计：	冯冯翼	
开　本：	660mm×960mm　1/16	
字　数：	237千字	
印　张：	10.5	
版　次：	2018年3月第2版	
印　次：	2022年1月第2次印刷	

出　版：	吉林出版集团股份有限公司
发　行：	吉林出版集团外语教育有限公司
地　址：	长春市福祉大路5788号龙腾国际大厦B座7层
电　话：	总编办：0431-81629929
	发行部：0431-81629927　0431-81629921(Fax)
印　刷：	北京一鑫印务有限责任公司

ISBN 978-7-5581-4731-9　定价：38.00元

前言 *PREFACE*

英国思想家培根说过：阅读使人深刻。阅读的真正目的是获取信息，开拓视野和陶冶情操。从语言学习的角度来说，学习语言若没有大量阅读就如隔靴搔痒，因为阅读中的语言是最丰富、最灵活、最具表现力、最符合生活情景的，同时读物中的情节、故事引人入胜，进而能充分调动读者的阅读兴趣，培养读者的文学修养，至此，语言的学习水到渠成。

"麦格希中英双语阅读文库"在世界范围内选材，涉及科普、社会文化、文学名著、传奇故事、成长励志等多个系列，充分满足英语学习者课外阅读之所需，在阅读中学习英语、提高能力。

◎难度适中

本套图书充分照顾读者的英语学习阶段和水平，从读者的阅读兴趣出发，以难易适中的英语语言为立足点，选材精心、编排合理。

◎精品荟萃

本套图书注重经典阅读与实用阅读并举。既包含国内外脍炙人口、耳熟能详的美文，又包含科普、人文、故事、励志类等多学科的精彩文章。

◎功能实用

本套图书充分体现了双语阅读的功能和优势，充分考虑到读者课外阅读的方便，超出核心词表的词汇均出现在使其意义明显的语境之中，并标注释义。

鉴于编者水平有限，凡不周之处，谬误之处，皆欢迎批评教正。

我们真心地希望本套图书承载的文化知识和英语阅读的策略对提高读者的英语著作欣赏水平和英语运用能力有所裨益。

丛书编委会

Contents

The Legend of Billy the Kid

Legend says that Billy the Kid killed one man for each of the 21 years of his life. That may or may not be true. Tales about this young *outlaw* are often *overblown*. It is hard to find the truth. Billy might have killed "only" 19 or as many as 27 men before he was gunned down in 1881. The

Not long before his violent death, young William Bonney—also known as Billy the Kid—posed for this picture. According to legend, Billy killed at least one man for each of his 21 years.

"小孩比利"的传奇故事

图片中的人物是不久前在暴力中已经去世的小孩比利，传说中，在他21岁的生命中，每年杀死一个人。

传说中，小孩比利在他21岁的生命中，每一年杀死一个人。这也许是真的，也许不是。这个传奇的故事经常被过度地夸张了。很难找出事实的真相。比利也许"只"杀死了19个人，也许杀死了27个人，直到1881年他被射杀。确切的数字并不重要。重要的是，比利在历史上如此出众的

---

outlaw *n.* 歹徒　　　　　　　　　　　　overblown *adj.* 夸张的

exact number is not important. What is important is the way Billy stands out in history. Hundreds of books have been written about him. Most picture him as a *romantic symbol* of the Old West. But in fact, he was a *heartless* killer.

Billy the Kid, also known as William Bonney, was born in New York City. When he was a young boy, his family moved to Silver City, New Mexico. Billy began his life of crime early. There was no school in his hometown of Silver City, New Mexico, so little Billy spent his time playing in the streets. He learned to gamble and to steal. He learned to fight with his *fists*. And he learned to use a gun.

The first man he killed was Frank Cahill. Apparently, Cahill called Billy a name. He was half joking. But Billy didn't think it was very funny. He hit Cahill. Then Cahill, a grown man, knocked 14-year-

---

方式。成百上千的书籍都写过他。大多数把他描绘成老西部的一个浪漫象征。但是，实际上他却是一个冷血杀手。

小孩比利也被称为威廉·波恩尼，出生在纽约市。当他还很小的时候，他们全家迁移到新墨西哥州的银城。比利的犯罪生涯开始得很早。他的家乡新墨西哥州银城没有学校，所以比利从小就在街头浪迹。他学会了赌博和盗窃，也学会了用拳头来打斗，进而学会了使用枪支。

他杀死的第一个人是佛朗克·卡希尔。很明显，卡希尔半开玩笑地骂了他一句。但是比利并不觉得他很有趣，并打了卡希尔。然后已经是成人的卡希尔把14岁的比利打倒在地上。这是一个错误。比利气急败坏，掏出了枪，将卡希尔击毙。

---

romantic *adj.* 浪漫的   symbol *n.* 象征；符号
heartless *adj.* 无情的   fist *n.* 拳头

old Billy to the ground. That was a mistake. *Flushed* with anger, Billy drew his gun and shot Cahill.

Billy was put in jail, but he escaped a few nights later. He became a *drifter.* From time to time, he worked as a cowboy. He also made money playing cards. One night Billy accused a fellow *gambler* of cheating. The man just laughed at Billy, calling him a "billy goat." A moment later, the man was lying dead on the floor with a bullet hole between his eyes.

Billy's real killing *spree* began in 1878. He was 19 years old. By then, he had hooked up with a man named John Tunstall. Tunstall, it was later said, was the Kid's one true friend. In fact, Billy called Tunstall "the only man that ever treated me [fairly]." Unfortunately, Tunstall had many enemies. One day a group of 25 men hunted him

---

比利被关进了监狱，但是几天之后他就逃走了，并成了一名流浪汉。他总是做牛仔，也通过玩牌来赚钱。一天晚上，比利指责他旁边的一名赌徒作弊。那个人嘲笑了比利，叫他"山羊比利"。一会儿工夫，那个人就躺在那里死了，双眼之间有一个弹孔。

比利真正的大开杀戒是从1878年开始的。当时他19岁，并同一个叫作约翰·坦斯塔尔的人交上了朋友。后来据说这个坦斯塔尔是比利唯一真正的朋友。实际上，比利称坦斯塔尔是"唯一一个[公正]对待我的人。"不幸的是坦斯塔尔有许多敌人。一天一伙25人将他击倒。他们冷酷地将他击毙。比利见证了这次谋杀，但是他距离这伙人太远了，没有能力阻止他

---

flush *v.* （因窘迫、愤怒等）（脸）发红
gambler *n.* 赌徒

drifter *n.* 流浪汉
spree *n.* 肆无忌惮的暴行

down. They shot him in cold blood. Billy *witnessed* the killing but was too far away to stop it. According to *legend*, Billy swore an oath at Tunstall's grave. "I'll get every [man] who helped kill John if it's the last thing I do."

Billy the Kid kept his word. He tracked down and shot every person who had played a part in Tunstall's death. One of these men was Sheriff William Brady. When Billy shot Brady, he gave himself a death sentence. He had killed a *lawman*. Now other lawmen came after him. They vowed to settle the score. Sheriff Pat Garrett tracked Billy for two years. In 1881 Garrett trapped him. Billy was arrested and brought to *trial*. He was found guilty of killing Brady. Judge Warren Bristol ordered Billy to be hanged until "you are dead, dead, dead."

们。按照传说，比利在坦斯塔尔的墓前发誓："我无论如何也要将那些参与杀害约翰的[人]杀掉。"

　　小孩比利信守着他的诺言。他跟踪并杀死了每一个在坦斯塔尔之死中起到作用的人。他们其中的一个人是治安官威廉·布兰迪。当比利击毙布兰迪时，他也给自己判处了死刑。比利杀害了一个执法人员。现在其他的执法人员开始追踪比利。他们发誓要将比利绳之以法。治安官帕特·加莱特用了两年的时间来跟踪比利。1881年，加莱特逮捕了他，并送他上了法庭。他被指控因为杀死布兰迪而有罪。法官华伦·布里斯托尔判决比利受绞刑，一直到"彻彻底底地死去。"

---

witness *v.* 目睹　　　　　　　　　　　legend *n.* 传说
lawman *n.* 执法者　　　　　　　　　　 trial *n.* 审讯

But again Billy the Kid escaped. Fifteen days before he was supposed to be hanged, Billy somehow got his hands on a gun. He shot his *guards*. Then he took off into the New Mexico wilderness.

Sheriff Garrett formed a *posse*. He went after Billy again. For three months, he stalked him. At last, Garrett got a tip. He heard that Billy was staying at the Maxwell *ranch* near the town of Fort Sumner. Just past midnight on July 14, 1881, Garrett slipped into Maxwell's bedroom off the front *porch*. Billy, hearing noises, walked down the porch. He peeked into Maxwell's dark room.

"Who's that?" the Kid called out.

Garrett answered with two shots. The first bullet struck Billy just above the heart. The Kid died on the spot. Sheriff Garrett rushed out of the room, shouting, "I killed the Kid! I killed the Kid!"

但是小孩比利又一次逃脱了。在比利绞刑日期前的15天，他拿起了一支枪。将警卫击毙。然后他逃往新墨西哥州的荒野。

治安官加莱特组织了一队人马，去追捕比利。三个月里，他一直在跟踪比利。最后，加莱特得到了一条线索。他听说比利藏在萨姆那堡附近的麦思维尔农场。1881年7月14日的午夜刚过，加莱特潜入了麦思维尔前门廊里面的卧室。比利听到了这个声音，他走下了门廊，向麦思维尔黑暗的卧室看了一眼。

"谁呀？"小孩喊道。

加莱特用两声枪响做出了回答。第一枪正击中比利心脏的上部。小孩当场死亡。治安官冲出了房间，大喊道："我宰了那个小子！我宰了那小子！"

---

guard *n.* 守卫 　　　　　　　　　　posse *n.* 一队
ranch *n.* 农场 　　　　　　　　　　porch *n.* 门廊

2

Bonnie and Clyde

He was the "Texas *Rattlesnake*." She was "*Suicide* Sal". Together they drove through Texas, *robbing* and killing at every turn. They never got rich. In fact, they never managed to steal more than $1,500 at any one time. But they left a trail of blood across the land. It was this *willingness* to

Early in their careers in crime, Bonnie Parker and Clyde Barrow took time out for some horseplay. In this picture, Bonnie pretends to rob Clyde at gunpoint.

邦尼和克莱德

在邦尼·帕克和克莱德·巴罗犯罪的早期,他们也有时间进行动手动脚、大声欢笑的玩闹。这张图片是邦尼假装使用枪支抢劫克莱德。

他是"得克萨斯响尾蛇",她是"自杀的小菜"。他们一起在得克萨斯旅行,每停一站就要抢劫、杀人。他们从来就没有真正富有过,他们从来就没试图盗窃过1500美元以上的财产。但是他们在路上留下了一连串的血迹。就是这种嗜杀性使邦尼和克莱德成名。从1932年4月至1934年5月,他们枪杀了12个人。

rattlesnake *n.* 响尾蛇
rob *v.* 抢劫

suicide *adj.* 自杀的
willingness *n.* 心甘情愿

kill that made Bonnie and Clyde famous. From April 1932 until May 1934, they shot and killed a *dozen* people.

Bonnie Parker met Clyde Barrow in 1930. She was a 19-year-old waitress who was bored with life. She wanted *excitement* and danger. That was exactly what 21-year-old Clyde seemed to offer. Clyde liked to gamble. He also liked to steal cars. When he needed money, he robbed stores or gas stations. Bonnie decided to *hook up* with him and have some "fun".

Unfortunately for Bonnie, Clyde wasn't a very good thief. At one break-in, he forgot to wear gloves. He left *fingerprints* all over the place. Soon after Bonnie met him, he was caught and sent to jail.

Bonnie could have walked away from Clyde right then. But she didn't. She was in love with him. So she visited him in jail, slipping

---

1930年邦尼·帕克和克莱德·巴罗相遇。当时她19岁，是一名女招待，她对生活很厌倦。她向往着刺激和危险。而这正是21岁的克莱德所能够提供的。克莱德喜欢赌博也喜欢偷车。当他缺钱时就抢劫商店和加油站。邦尼决定和他在一起，找些"乐趣"。

对于邦尼来说，不幸的是，克莱德并不是一个很在行的窃贼。在一次入室盗窃中，他忘记了戴手套，所以留下了很多的手印。邦尼遇到他没有多久，他就被捕关进了监狱。

邦尼本来可以马上从他身边走开。但是邦尼没有这么做，她爱上了克莱德。所以她去探望了监狱中的克莱德，把用胶带粘在大腿上带进去的

---

dozen n. 十二个；一打
hook up 搭上关系

excitement n. 兴奋；刺激
fingerprint n. 指纹

him a gun that she had taped to her leg. That night, Clyde broke out of jail. He was quickly *recaptured*, however, and sent to Eastman, one of the toughest prisons in the country. Clyde served two years there. When he got out, he was angry and *bitter*. He vowed never to spend another day in prison. "I'll die first," he *declared*.

Clyde meant what he said. With Bonnie at his side, he began robbing again. But now he was tougher. In fact, he was *ruthless*. He carried guns wherever he went. And he was ready to use them. On April 28, 1932, Clyde robbed a jewelry store in Hillsboro, Texas. He still wasn't a very smooth criminal, however, and during the robbery he panicked. He shot the 65-year-old owner through the heart.

Now Clyde was a murderer as well as a thief. Still, Bonnie remained loyal to him. In fact, she became as cold and hard as

一支枪偷偷地给了他。那天晚上，克莱德越狱了。很快他就再次被抓，然后被送到了伊斯特曼监狱，这是全国戒备最森严的监狱。克莱德在那里服刑两年。出狱时，他变得愤怒而且刻薄。他发誓再也不进监狱待上一天。"我宁可先死，"他宣称道。

克莱德真的是这样做的。邦尼成为他的帮凶，他又开始了抢劫生涯。而且现在克莱德变得心狠手辣，也可以说是毫无顾忌。不论到哪里他都带着枪支，并时刻准备使用。1932年4月28日，克莱德抢劫了得克萨斯希思博罗镇的一家珠宝店。但是他的手法并不老道，在抢劫过程中他害怕了，并开枪击中了65岁店主的心脏。

现在克莱德拥有了杀人犯和窃贼的双重身份。但是邦尼还是忠于他。实际上她也变得和克莱德一样的冷酷无情。对于她来说，杀人成为一种游

recapture *v.* 再捕获
declare *v.* 宣称；断言

bitter *adj.* 愤怒的；怀恨的
ruthless *adj.* 无情的；残忍的

he was. To her, killing became a kind of joke. She had Clyde take pictures of her holding a machine gun. In one photo, she pretended to be robbing Clyde. In another, she and Clyde were both holding *pistols* and *grinning* wildly.

Like Clyde, Bonnie figured she would die young. She fully expected to be shot full of police bullets someday. That attitude earned her the nickname Suicide Sal. Bonnie actually wrote a poem by that title. The poem told the story of a woman who fell in love with a "*professional* killer." One part read:

I couldn't help loving him madly;

For him even now I would die.

Bonnie also wrote a poem called "The Story of Bonnie and Clyde." It included these lines:

They don't think they're too tough or desperate,

戏。她让克莱德给她拍一张端着机关枪的照片。一张照片上她假装抢劫克莱德，另一张，她和克莱德都手持枪支，哈哈大笑。

和克莱德一样，邦尼知道她将死得很年轻。她完全做好了某一天被警察扫射击毙的准备。这种态度使她获得"自杀的小菜"的外号。实际上，邦尼使用这个名字写了一首小诗。这首诗讲述了一个女人爱上了一名"职业杀手"。其中一句是这样的：

我禁不住疯狂地爱上他；

为了他，我宁可付出自己的一切。

邦尼还写了一首叫作"邦尼和克莱德的故事"的诗。其中有如下的段落：

他们并不认为自己

---

pistol *n.* 手枪   grin *v.* 露齿而笑
professional *adj.* 职业的   desperate *adj.* 不顾一切；令人绝望的

They know that the law

always wins;

They've been shot at before,

But they do not ignore

That death is the wages of sin.

By the spring of 1933, Bonnie and Clyde had murdered seven people. They killed an old shopkeeper for $28. Clyde killed a *sheriff* and a *deputy* who spoke to him at a *barn* dance. Clyde shot one man on Christmas Day just so he could take a ride in the man's car.

That June, Bonnie and Clyde were traveling down a country road. Clyde was driving. He was usually an excellent driver. But on this day, he failed to see that a bridge was closed for repairs. He tried to stop at the last minute, but it was too late. The car flew over a steep

---

过于残酷和绝望，

他们知道

天网恢恢，疏而不漏；

他们冒过枪林弹雨，

但是他们并不否认

死亡是罪恶的报酬。

到1933年春季为止，邦尼和克莱德已经杀害了7个人。他们为了28美元而杀死了一名年老的店主。克莱德杀死了一名治安官和一名副长官，因为他们在一次谷仓舞会中跟他说话。克莱德在圣诞节杀了一名男子，原因只是想开他的车。

在6月，邦尼和克莱德在一段乡村公路上驾车行驶，克莱德开车。他

---

sin *n.* 罪恶

deputy *n.* 副职；众议员

sheriff *n.* 地方司法官

barn *n.* 谷仓

bank, crashed, and exploded in a ball of fire. Clyde was thrown clear of the wreck. Bonnie, however, was trapped in the flames. By the time Clyde pulled her out, her whole body was badly burned.

Clyde took her to a nearby farmhouse. There a farmer's wife *bandaged* Bonnie as best she could. But Bonnie was in terrible pain. For a while, it looked as though she might die. Clyde nursed Bonnie all summer. He also continued to rob and kill. He rounded up some other *thugs* to help him. One was his brother Buck.

That July, Buck was killed in a shoot-out with police. It happened at a park where the outlaws were *camping*. Clyde and Bonnie were there, too, but they managed to escape. Although Clyde was hit with four bullets, he did not fall. He helped Bonnie swim across a river. Then he stole a car and whisked her up into the hills.

是一个相当不错的驾驶员。但是在这段路上，他没有看到桥梁已经封闭维修。他尽力想停下来，但是太晚了。汽车滑下了陡峭的河岸，撞击并爆炸成了一团火球。克莱德被抛到车体的外面。但是邦尼被困在了大火里。当克莱德把她从车里拉出来时，她全身已经严重烧伤。

克莱德把她带到附近的一间农舍。农夫的妻子尽可能地包扎了邦尼。但是邦尼浑身疼痛得厉害。这段时间看起来她好像是要死了。这个夏天，克莱德都在照料邦尼。同时，他也继续着抢劫和杀人。他网罗了一些歹徒来帮助他。其中一个是他的兄弟巴克。

那年的7月，巴克在与警察的交火中丧生。这是在歹徒们的栖身之地，一个公园里面发生的。克莱德和邦尼也在那里。虽然克莱德身中4枪，但是他没有倒下。他帮助邦尼游过了小河。然后偷了一辆车，接上邦尼跑上山。

---

bandage *v.* 用绷带包扎

camp *v.* 临时安顿；暂住

thug *n.* 暴徒

Bonnie and Clyde spent the next few weeks in *misery*. Both of them needed medical attention. But they didn't dare go to a hospital. So, as Bonnie put it, "we lived in little *ravines, secluded* woods, down side roads for days that stretched into weeks. We were ... so sick that time went by without our knowing it. We lost track of the days."

By September, Clyde was feeling better. He took Bonnie to visit her mother, Emma Parker. Mrs. Parker was *horrified* by her daughter's appearance. She said, "Bonnie was ... unable to walk without help. She was miserably thin and looked much older. Her leg was drawn up under her. Her body was covered in scars."

Time was clearly running out for Bonnie and Clyde. Winter came. Still, the couple often had to sleep out in the open or in

---

以后的几个星期，邦尼和克莱德在痛苦中度过。他们都需要医疗救治。但是他们不敢到医院去。所以就如邦尼所说，"我们生活在小溪谷里、隐蔽的树丛里、路边的沟壑里，一待就是几个星期。我们……病得很厉害，已经完全没有了时间观念。每一天都不知道怎么过的。"

到9月份时，克莱德觉得好一些了。他带着邦尼去看望了一下她的妈妈，爱玛·帕克。帕克夫人被她女儿的样子吓坏了。她说："没有人的帮助……邦尼不能走路。她瘦弱得可怕，看起来要比实际年龄老得多。她的腿无力地下垂着，而且身上布满伤疤。"

给邦尼和克莱德留下的时间越来越少了。冬天来了。而这对年轻人还

---

misery *n.* 痛苦
secluded *adj.* 隐蔽的

ravine *n.* 沟壑
horrify *v.* 使震惊

their unheated car. They moved from place to place, sticking to backwoods and small towns. By now, though, they weren't safe anywhere. A lawman named Frank Hamer was closing in on them.

In May of 1934, Hamer and his men set up an *ambush* near Gibland, Louisiana. On May 24, Bonnie and Clyde *approached* in a stolen car. Hamer's men shouted at them to halt. Said one officer, "We wished to give them a chance."

"But," added Hamer, "They both reached for their guns."

Before Bonnie or Clyde could get off a shot, officers *blasted* them with a total of 187 bullets.

Clyde slumped in his seat, dead. Bonnie, too, died *instantly*. The car crashed into a hillside. When Hamer and his men got to it, they found a machine gun lying in Bonnie's lap. Clyde's hand still rested

---

要在露天睡觉或者在没有取暖装置的车子里面睡。他们从一个地方跑到另一个地方，待在偏僻的林地或者小城镇中。现在他们不再安全了。一个叫作佛朗克·海默的警官正在逼近他们。

1934年5月，海默和他的队伍在路易斯安那州的吉伯兰设置了埋伏。5月24日邦尼和克莱德驾驶一辆偷来的车接近了这里。海默的人向他们喊话，让他们停下。一名警察说："我们希望给他们一个机会。"

"但是，"海默说，"他们两个人都掏出了枪。"

在邦尼和克莱德能够开枪之前，警察猛烈开火，其中187枚子弹击中了两人。

克莱德瘫坐在椅子上，死了。邦尼也马上就死了。汽车撞到了路边的

---

ambush *n.* 埋伏　　　　　　　approach *v.* 接近
blast *v.* 爆炸；进攻　　　　　instantly *adv.* 立即；马上

on a sawed-off shotgun.

In the end, then, Bonnie Parker had been right. She had *predicted* this day would come. Her *poem* called "The Story of Bonnie and Clyde" *concluded* with these words:

Some day they'll go down together;

And they'll bury them side by side;

To a few it'll be grief—

To the law a relief—

But it's death for Bonnie and Clyde.

山壁。当海默和他的人赶到附近时，他们发现邦尼的腿上有一挺机关枪。克莱德的手还放在那支锯掉了枪管的步枪上。

　　最终，证明邦尼·帕克是对的。她已经预料到她末日的到来。她的诗"邦尼和克莱德的故事"中有这样的诗句：

　　有一天

　　他们会一齐倒下；

　　他们会把他们并排埋葬；

　　对于一些人来说是悲惨——

　　对于法律，这是解脱——

　　但，这就是邦尼和克莱德之死。

---

predict *v.* 预计；预料　　　　　　　　　　　　poem *n.* 诗

conclude *v.* 作结论

3

Izzy and Moe

They had funny names: Izzy and Moe. And these two guys really were funny! People around the country laughed when they read about Izzy and Moe's latest tricks. It seemed that each new *stunt* was funnier than the last one. But Izzy and Moe were not a *circus* act or a *comedy* team. They

During Prohibition, when making and selling liquor became illegal, bootleggers feared government agents. Izzy Einstein and Moe Smith, the stout gentlemen on either side of this illegal still, were two of the flashiest agents.

里奇和莫尔

在《禁酒令》发布之后，酒的制造和销售成为非法，酿私酒的人害怕政府调查人员。在这个非法蒸酒器的两边站着的就是里奇·爱因斯坦和莫尔·史密斯，他们是侦查这种非法行为的侦探，两人很显眼。

他们的名字很好笑，里奇和莫尔。而且两个人也真是很好玩！当全国的人们读到他们最新的计策时都会哈哈大笑。但是里奇和莫尔不是马戏团的演员或者喜剧搭档。他们是警察。

stunt *n.* 噱头；手腕　　　　　　　　circus *n.* 马戏团
comedy *n.* 喜剧

were cops.

In 1919 a new law was passed. The law made it *illegal* to *manufacture*, sell, or transport *liquor*. This law was canceled in 1933. But for 14 years, people were not allowed to use liquor. That meant beer and wine were out.

So were *gin*, whiskey, and all other drinks containing alcohol. This time period was called Prohibition. That's because people were prohibited from having alcohol.

Many people ignored the new law. They thought it was wrong. They said the government had no right to deny them a bottle of beer or a glass of wine. Some people smuggled liquor into the country. These people were called bootleggers. Other people made their own booze—liquor—at home. "Bathtub gin" became a favorite. And all

---

1919年通过了一个新的法令。新法宣布制造、销售、运输酒类饮料是非法的。这个法令在1933年取消了。但是在此14年间，人们不允许使用酒。也就是说连啤酒和葡萄酒都不行。

禁止的还有杜松子酒、威士忌和所有含有酒精的饮料。因为人们禁止饮酒，所以这个历史时期叫作"禁酒时期"。

许多人对这个新法视而不见，而且认为新法是错误的。他们说政府没有权力否定他们的一杯啤酒、一杯葡萄酒。一些人把酒走私进入美国。这些人叫作"私酒贩子"。另一些人在自己家酿酒。"浴缸杜松子酒"成为一种时尚。而且在整个美国，人们偷偷进入一种叫作"小心！"的地下酒

---

illegal *adj.* 非法的

liquor *n.* 酒；含酒精饮料

manufacture *v.* 制造

gin *n.* 杜松子酒

over America, people slipped into illegal bars called speakeasies. Customers had to "speak easy" so they would not *attract* the attention of the police.

The police, meanwhile, were trying to *enforce* the law. That's where Izzy and Moe came in. Izzy Einstein and Moe Smith were government agents. Their job was to find people serving or drinking liquor and to arrest them. To do this, Izzy and Moe *dressed in* disguises. Some of their *costumes* were quite outrageous. They used smiles and laughs in order to trap bar owners. They were friendly with everyone—until it was time to make an arrest!

One night Izzy and Moe dressed up as football players. They knocked on a speakeasy door in New York City. "We won the game!"they shouted. "Let us in. We want to celebrate with a pint [of beer]."

馆。顾客们要小心不引起警察的注意。

当时警方努力地执行这项法律。里奇和莫尔在这时出现了。里奇·爱因斯坦和莫尔·史密斯就是政府的调查人员。他们的工作就是找到偷着卖酒的和偷着买酒的人，并把他们逮捕。为了这样做，里奇和莫尔使用了一些伪装。他们的一些伪装甚至可以说是出乎意料的。他们使用微笑和欢笑来使店主上当。他们对任何人都很友好——直到执行逮捕任务的时候！

一天晚上，里奇和莫尔打扮成橄榄球运动员的样子。他们敲响纽约市的一家地下酒馆的门。"我们赢了！"他们喊道，"让我们进去，我们要庆祝一下，喝上一杯[啤酒]！"

---

attract *v.* 吸引；引起
dress in 乔装打扮

enforce *v.* 实施；使生效
costume *n.* 服装；装束

The bar owner laughed and let them in. He praised them for their *victory*. Then he got them each a beer. But his smile quickly *faded* when Izzy and Moe flashed their badges. The two agents arrested the man for serving them liquor.

Then there was the time Izzy and Moe wore dresses. Pretending to be ladies who had just come from the theater, they entered a restaurant. The two "ladies" ordered a small meal. All the time, their eyes *scanned* the restaurant. Izzy and Moe were looking for signs that the owner was selling liquor. They found plenty of *clues*. The next day, police raided the place. They found more than $10,000 worth of smuggled liquor.

Once Izzy and Moe dressed up as car mechanics. They found 200 cases of whiskey in a garage. One time they dressed as

---

店主笑了，让他们进来，并赞扬了他们的胜利。店主给他们每人倒了一杯啤酒。但是他的笑容马上褪了下去，因为里奇和莫尔亮出了他们的警徽。两名侦探以提供酒的名义逮捕了店主。

有时，里奇和莫尔也穿上裙子。假装是刚刚从剧场出来的女士，他们进入饭店。两位"女士"点了一些食物。他们的眼睛却一直在扫视着整个饭店。里奇和莫尔在观察店主卖酒的蛛丝马迹。他们找到了足够的证据。第二天警方袭击了这个地方。他们发现了价值10,000美元的走私酒。

一次，里奇和莫尔装扮成了汽车机械师。他们在一家汽修厂找到了200箱的威士忌。一次他们化妆成掘墓人，袭击了墓地附近的一家酒吧。

---

victory *n.* 胜利

scan *v.* 仔细检查

fade *v.* 褪去

clue *n.* 线索

gravediggers and raided a bar near a graveyard. Once they put on long black coats and carried violin cases. Their target? A bar that served only musicians. At times they also posed as horse traders, farmers, and rabbis.

Izzy and Moe's fame spread rapidly. "Be careful," bar owners would warn each other. "Izzy and Moe are in the *neighborhood*." Most owners came to hate these two agents.

Once Izzy walked into a bar alone. He looked up and saw his own photograph *hanging over* the bar. The owner had put black cloth around it to show that he wished Izzy were dead. Izzy went ahead and ordered a drink. It must not have been a very good photo of him, because the *bartender* didn't recognize him. Still, the man wouldn't pour Izzy a drink.

还有一次他们穿上了黑色的大衣，背上了小提琴盒。他们的目标？是一个专门为音乐家服务的酒吧。有时，他们也装扮成马贩子，农夫和犹太牧师。

里奇和莫尔的名气传播得很快。"小心！"酒吧的店主互相警告着，"里奇和莫尔就在附近。"大部分的店主开始对这两名侦探怀恨在心。

有一次里奇自己一个人走进了一家酒吧。他抬头看到他的照片被挂在酒吧的正中。店主在照片的周围裹上了黑布，表示希望里奇死掉。里奇走上前去，要了一杯酒。这张照片一定照得不好，因为酒吧的招待没有认出他来。而且还倒了一杯酒给他。

---

gravedigger *n.* 挖墓者
hang over 悬挂在……上

neighborhood *n.* 附近
bartender *n.* 酒吧侍者

"I don't know you," the bartender said. (In those days, bartenders often refused to serve people they didn't know. They were worried about being caught by agents like Izzy and Moe.)

"Sure you know me," Izzy said. "I'm Izzy Epstein, the famous agent."

"You don't even have the name right," the bartender said with a laugh. "That guy's name is Einstein."

Izzy *insisted* that the name was Epstein. At last, he offered to bet the bartender a drink about it. The bartender agreed. He *poured* out two drinks. To settle the bet, Izzy *pulled out* his badge. He arrested the bartender on the spot.

Izzy and Moe came to the end of the line in 1925. They were *dismissed* from their jobs. The reason isn't clear. At the time, their

---

　　"我不认识你，"招待员说。（在那时，招待经常拒绝给他们不认识的人倒酒。他们担心遇到像里奇和莫尔那样的侦探。）

　　"你一定认识我，"里奇说，"我是里奇·爱普斯坦，著名的侦探。"

　　"你连名字都没有说对，"招待嘲笑着说，"那个家伙的名字是爱因斯坦。"

　　里奇坚持说名字是爱普斯坦。最后他和招待打赌，赌一杯酒。招待同意了。他倒了两杯酒。为了赢得赌注，里奇掏出了警徽，并当场将招待逮捕。

　　里奇和莫尔一直工作到1925年。他们被解雇了，原因不明。当时，

---

insist v. 坚持
pull out 取出；出示

pour v. 倒；灌
dismiss v. 开除

bosses said Izzy and Moe had become too famous. Too many people *recognized* them. That meant they were no longer as useful as they had once been.

That might not have been the real reason. Some other agents *resented* Izzy and Moe's success. Still other agents feared their honesty. After all, some agents were *crooks*. They were paid by *bootleggers* to look the other way. Perhaps these crooked agents thought Izzy and Moe would find out about their deals. These agents might have arranged to get Izzy and Moe fired.

In any case, Izzy and Moe had built up quite a record. In four years, they arrested more than 4,000 people. They also destroyed more than five million bottles of liquor!

他们的老总说，里奇和莫尔太出名了。太多的人认识他们。也就是说他们不再像以前那么有用了。

这可能不是真正的原因。其他的一些侦探嫉妒里奇和莫尔的成功。另一些人害怕他们的忠诚。毕竟有一些侦探本身就是坏人。他们接受私酒贩子的贿赂来从另一个角度照看他们。可能这些坏侦探觉得里奇和莫尔可能会发现他们的交易。可能是这些侦探私下安排了他们解雇的事件。

无论怎样，里奇和莫尔都可以说创造了一个纪录。在四年里，他们逮捕了4000人。他们也毁掉了五百多万瓶酒。

---

recognize *v.* 认识　　　　　　resent *v.* 怨恨
crook *n.* 恶棍；骗子　　　　　bootlegger *n.* 造私酒者

Kidnapped!

Italian police thought it was a *hoax*. They did not believe 16-year-old John Paul Getty III had been *kidnapped*. A *ransom* note had been sent to Getty's mother. But it did not *convince* them. The note read:

Dear Mother,

I have fallen into the hands of

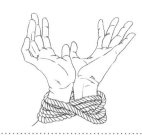

At first no one believed that John Paul Getty III, grandson of the richest man in the world, had been kidnapped. Then a grisly envelope arrived, and everything changed.

遭遇绑架！

起初，没有人相信约翰·保罗·盖蒂三世，世界上最富有的人的孙子被人绑架了。但是当一封可怕的信到来时，一切都变了。

起初，意大利警方认为这是一起恶作剧。他们不相信16岁的约翰·保罗·盖蒂三世被绑架了。盖蒂的母亲收到了一张勒索赎金的便条。但是这并没有使他们相信。这张便条上面写着：

亲爱的妈妈：

我被绑架了。

hoax *n.* 骗局；恶作剧

ransom *n.* 赎金

kidnap *v.* 绑架

convince *v.* 使信服

kidnappers. Don't let me be killed!

Make sure that the police do not

interfere. You must absolutely not take this as a joke.

The note then *demanded* $17 million for the boy's safe return.

Police had reasons to be *dubious*. Getty's grandfather was the richest man in the world. Yet young Paul was always running out of money. Neither his father nor his grandfather would give him the cash he wanted. Paul himself had never earned any money on his own. He had dropped out of high school. He had no job. His idea of a tough day was going to a big party. Just before he disappeared, he joked about his *lack of funds*. He knew of a way to solve his money problems, he told friends with a laugh. All he had to do was stage his own "perfect kidnapping".

我不想死！

不要让警察参与进来。

千万不要认为这是一次玩笑。

便条最后要求支付1700万美元换回这个男孩。

警方有足够的原因表示怀疑。盖蒂的祖父是世界上最富有的人。但是小保罗却总是缺钱花。他的父亲和爷爷都不给他想要的现金。保罗自己也从来没有赚过钱。他从高中退学了，而且没有工作。他最害怕的事情就是去参加大型的聚会。就在他消失之前，还开玩笑说他缺少资金。保罗知道一种解决自己金钱问题的方法，他开着玩笑地告诉他的朋友们，他所要做的就是自导自演一个"完美的绑架"。

---

demand *v.* 要求

lack of 缺乏

dubious *adj.* 可疑的

fund *n.* 资金

That explains why police were not too alarmed when he disappeared on July 10, 1973. They did *investigate*, of course. They looked around. They asked a few questions. But *privately* they thought the whole thing had been set up by Paul. They waited to see what Grandfather Getty would do. Would he come up with money to "save" his missing grandson?

Old Mr. Getty answered that question right away. "I'm against paying any money," he snapped. "It only *encourages* kidnappers." These words upset Gail Getty, mother of the missing boy. She believed her son was in real danger. "At first I thought it might be a stupid joke," she told one person. "But then I understood it was *serious*." With old Mr. Getty refusing to help, Gail feared her son might soon be killed. She announced that she would try to raise the

---

这就是为什么1973年7月10日他消失时，警方并没有过于紧张。当然他们也的确做了一些调查。他们四处看看，而且问了一些问题。但是私下里警方认为整个事件就是保罗自己设计的。他们等待着看盖蒂爷爷要怎么办。他是不是要出钱来"救"他的孙子？

盖蒂老先生马上回答了。"我反对支付赎金，"他打着响指说，"那只能鼓励绑匪。"这席话使失踪男孩的母亲盖尔·盖蒂很恼火。她相信她的孩子真的是遇到危险了。"开始时，我以为这可能是个愚蠢的玩笑，"她告诉另一个人说，"但然后我明白了这是真的危险。"盖蒂老先生拒绝帮助，盖尔害怕她的孩子可能很快会被杀掉。便宣称她将尽力筹集赎金。

---

investigate *v.* 调查   privately *adv.* 私下地
encourage *v.* 鼓励   serious *adj.* 严肃的；认真的

ransom money herself.

But Gail did not have that kind of cash. She was *divorced* from John Paul Getty, Jr. So she couldn't get her hands on the Getty *fortune*. Meanwhile, her ex-husband agreed with his father. No money would be paid out.

The weeks *dragged by*. Then, in November, something happened that changed everything. An envelope was sent to an Italian newspaper. When employees opened it, they found a *gruesome* sight. The envelope contained a note, a lock of Paul's red hair, and a human ear.

"This is Paul's first ear," read the note. "If within 10 days the family still believes that this is a joke mounted by him, then the other ear will arrive. In other words, he will arrive in little bits."

但是，盖尔没有那么多钱。她和小约翰·保罗·盖蒂离婚了，所以她不能动盖蒂的财产。而且她的前夫与前夫的父亲一致拒绝支付金钱。

一个星期又一个星期过去了。在11月发生的事情改变了这一切。一家意大利的报馆收到了一个信封。当报馆的工作人员打开信封时，他们发现了一个可怕的情景。信封里面有一张便条、一束保罗的红头发和一只人耳朵。

"这是保罗的第一只耳朵，"纸条上写道，"如果十天之内，他的家庭还是相信这是小保罗设计的玩笑的话，另一只耳朵就会寄到。换句话说，他将一块一块地来到你们身边。"

---

divorce *v.* 离婚
drag by 慢慢度过

fortune *n.* 财富
gruesome *adj.* 可怕的

Medical experts checked out the ear. It was Paul's. The boy's father and grandfather were shocked. They now realized that the kidnapping was real. Fearing for Paul's life, they agreed to bargain with the kidnappers. They would not pay $17 million, they said. But they would hand over $2.8 million.

The kidnappers took that deal. They told the Getty family to put the money in three *plastic bags*. These bags were to be left along the side of a road in southern Italy. The Gettys did this. But first they had the police *photograph* each bill. That way the money could be traced. After the ransom money was *delivered*, the Gettys sat back to wait. They hoped and *prayed* that Paul would be returned to them.

On December 14, Gail Getty got a late-night phone call from the

---

医学专家检查了这只耳朵。它是保罗的。孩子的父亲和祖父都十分震惊。现在他们意识到绑架是真的，而且害怕保罗有生命危险，同意和绑架者谈判。他们无法提供1700万美元，他们说，他们可以提供280万美元。

绑架者们接受了这个方案。他们让盖蒂家人把钱装在三个塑料袋子里面。这些袋子要放到意大利南部的道路旁边。盖蒂的家人这样做了。但是警方首先影印了每一张钞票。这样可以追查它们的行踪。盖蒂一家把赎金投放完毕后，便回家等候。他们希望并且祷告保罗能够平安回来。

12月14日，盖尔·盖蒂在接近午夜时接到绑架者的电话。他们说，

---

plastic bag 塑料袋　　　　　　　　photograph *v.* 拍照
deliver *v.* 递送　　　　　　　　pray *v.* 祈祷

kidnappers. They had received the money, they said. They were about to *release* her son. Early the next morning, a truck driver named Antonio Tedesco saw a young man standing by the side of the road. It was raining hard. Yet the young man was not wearing a raincoat. He was standing in wet clothes, waving his arms wildly. Tedesco slowed down. He saw that the young man was crying. As Tedesco pulled to a stop, the youth staggered over to the truck.

"I am Paul Getty," he said.

And so, five months after being kidnapped, John Paul Getty III was free. It turned out that he had suffered greatly during his five months as a *hostage*. The kidnappers had kept him *blindfolded* most of the time. They had forced him to march from one mountain hideout to the next. These long *treks* had exhausted him. Cold, frightened, and

---

他们收到了钱，将释放她的孩子。第二天拂晓，一个名叫安东尼奥·特德思科的卡车司机发现路边站着一个男孩。天正下着暴雨。但是这个男孩没有穿雨衣。他身上的衣服湿透了，近乎疯狂地挥舞着手臂。特德思科减慢了速度。他看到男孩正在哭泣。特德思科停了下来，年轻人蹒跚着走到卡车前面。

"我是保罗·盖蒂，"他说。

这样在被绑架5个月后，约翰·保罗·盖蒂三世自由了。后来发现他在被囚禁的5个月中受到了极大的折磨。绑架者们大部分的时间用黑布蒙住了他的眼睛。他们逼着他从一个山洞走到另一个山洞。长长的山路使他

---

release *v.* 释放
blindfolded *adj.* 被蒙上眼睛的

hostage *n.* 人质
trek *n.* 艰苦跋涉；徒步旅程

poorly fed, he had grown very weak.

Worst of all had been the ear *episode*. The kidnappers had tried to knock him out before they cut off his ear. "They struck me on the head to make me *unconscious*," he said. "But I felt everything. It was terrible."

With Paul safe, the police turned their attention to catching the kidnappers. *Undercover* officers had seen men pick up the ransom money. So the police knew who the kidnappers were.

In late January 1974, police made their move. They arrested all eight kidnappers. And so the kidnappers did not get to enjoy much of the Getty money. It had been the highest ransom ever paid in Italy. But as these kidnappers discovered, they had to *return* the money and go to jail.

筋疲力尽。寒冷、恐惧、缺少食物使他十分虚弱。

最糟糕的还是耳朵事件。绑架者们在割下他耳朵之前试图打昏他。"他们打了我的头部想打昏我，"他说，"但是我感受到了这一切，太可怕了。"

保罗已经安全了，警方开始抓捕绑架者。便衣警察看到有人拿走了赎金，所以知道绑架者是谁。

1974年1月下旬，警方出动了。他们逮捕了所有的8个人。大多数盖蒂的钱款还没有来得及挥霍。这是意大利曾支付过的最高的赎金。但是那些绑架者们也发现，他们要归还这些钱款，而且还要坐牢。

---

episode *n.* （组成一个较大事件的）一个事件　　　　unconscious *adj.* 无意识的
undercover *adj.* 秘密的　　　　　　　　　　　　　　return *v.* 返回

5

The Brink's Robbery

Joseph "Big Joe" McGinnis dreamed of *committing* the perfect crime. In 1948 he hooked up with Tony "Fats" Pino. Pino shared McGinnis's dream. Together, these two longtime criminals set to work. They spent two years planning a *flawless robbery*. Nothing would be left

Brink's armored trucks such as this one, filled with cash on the way to vaults, have been the targets of many robbers. But one gang didn't stop at just the money in a single truck. They went straight to Brink's headquarters.

布林克的抢劫

　　这一辆是布林克装甲车，是用来向金库运输现金用的，一直是许多劫匪的目标。但是一伙劫匪并没有止于一辆车里面的金钱，他们直接去了布林克的总部。

　　"大乔"约瑟夫·麦克吉尼斯梦想着做一次完美的打劫。1948年，他结识了"胖子"托尼·皮诺。皮诺也有麦克吉尼斯的打算。两名长期的罪犯开始合作。他们用了两年的时间设计了一次完美的抢劫计划。不会发生任何意外。不会遗漏下任何证据。而且如果一切正常，他们都可以成为富人。

commit *v.* 干（坏事）；犯（罪）　　　　　　　　flawless *adj.* 完美的
robbery *n.* 抢劫

to chance. No *evidence* would be left behind. And, if all went well, they would both end up rich.

The two thieves picked a tough target to rob—the Brink's Company in Boston. Brink's is an *armored* car service. It sends steel-plated cars to pick up money from stores around town. The armored cars take the money to Brink's *headquarters*. There it is counted, sorted, and held until the stores need it again. In 1950, as much as $10 million a day flowed through the Brink's office.

McGinnis and Pino planned their robbery with great care. They picked nine other men to join them. These were not just any nine men. Each brought a special skill to the group. Some, *for instance*, were good drivers or sharp lookout men. Also, seven of the men had to be the same size. McGinnis and Pino chose men who were about

---

　　两个劫匪选择了一个硬骨头去打劫——位于波士顿的布林克公司。布林克公司提供装甲车服务。它派出装有钢甲的车到整个城市的商铺去取钱。装甲车把钱送到布林克的总部。金钱在这里被点数，分类保存，直到这些商店再次需要。在1950年，每天布林克办公室经手的现金达1000万。

　　麦克吉尼斯和皮诺极其小心地策划了他们的计划。另外又选择了9个人来入伙。他们可不是普普通通的9个人，他们都身怀绝技。比如，有的是技术高超的驾驶员或者目光敏锐的望风者。而且他们中的7个人身高相同。麦克吉尼斯和皮诺选择个头大约5英尺9英寸，体重大约170至180磅

---

evidence *n.* 证据
headquarters *n.* 总部

armored *adj.* 装甲的
for instance 举例来说

five feet nine inches tall and weighed between 170 and 180 pounds. These men would be the ones to enter the Brink's office and bring out the money. They would all dress alike. They would wear the same scary *masks*, rubber-soled shoes, gloves, coats, and caps. That would make it hard for the Brink's guards to *identify* them. (McGinnis would be one of the seven, but Pino was too heavy for the job. He agreed to stay with the getaway truck.)

Robbing the Brink's headquarters would not be easy. The place was full of steel *vaults* and armed guards. McGinnis and Pino knew this. So they took plenty of time. They studied the *layout* of the building. They found out when the guards were on duty and where they were stationed. They watched the money flow in and out of the office. They knew when the big money was there.

的人。他们负责进入布林克的办公室并带出钱来。他们的穿着完全相同，而且戴着相同的，吓人的面具，穿着完全一样的胶底鞋、手套、上衣和帽子。布林克的警卫很难分辨他们。（麦克吉尼斯是七个人之一，但是皮诺太胖了，他同意待在逃跑用的卡车里面。）

打劫布林克总部可不是一件容易的事情。这个地方充满了钢铁的金库和武装的警卫。麦克吉尼斯和皮诺知道这些。所以他们花费了很长的时间研究了建筑的布局。他们查找出警卫什么时候当班，驻扎在哪里，并监视着现金进入和运出办公室，知道什么时候大笔现金会在这里。

---

mask *n.* 面具
vault *n.* 金库；保险库

identify *v.* 辨认；认出
layout *n.* 布局

One of the toughest problems they faced was the locks. The gang had to pass through five locked doors to get from the street to the Brink's office. McGinnis and Pino came up with a bold plan. Late one night, a few of the gang members slipped into the building. One of them, a professional *locksmith*, removed the lock on the first door. He took it away and quickly made a key for it. Then—that same night—he hurried back to the Brink's building. He got the lock back in place before anyone noticed it was missing.

The robbers returned on four other nights. Each time they *repeated* their *actions*. They made keys for the locks on the four other doors. Now they would be able to walk right into the Brink's office. There, they knew, they would find guards standing inside a wire cage. That was where all the money was.

他们面临最困难的问题是锁。他们一伙需要通过五道锁住的大门才能从大街上进入布林克的办公室。麦克吉尼斯和皮诺想出来一个大胆的计划。一天深夜，他们一些同伙溜进大楼。他们其中的一个是高超的锁匠，取下了第一个门上的锁。他把它拿走，马上配了一把钥匙。然后——还在同一天晚上——他又回到布林克的大楼。在有人意识到锁头丢失之前再把它安装好。

劫匪们又来了四个晚上。每一次他们都重复着。他们为其他四个门也都配了钥匙。现在他们能直接进入布林克的办公室了。他们知道，在那里将看到铁丝笼子里面的警卫。那里就是金库。

---

locksmith *n.* 锁匠
action *n.* 行动

repeat *v.* 重复

Next, McGinnis and Pino made the gang practice the robbery. More than 20 times, the thieves slipped into the building. They used their keys to unlock door after door. Each time, they got right up to the *innermost* door. Then they turned and left.

At last, McGinnis and Pino decided they were ready for the real thing. On January 17, 1950, they gave the *signal*. That night, a little before seven o'clock, the men took their places. Seven of them put on masks and sneaked into the building. They opened the five locked doors. At 7:10 p.m., they opened the innermost door. They were in the Brink's office. There, as expected, they saw five guards. The guards were all inside the wire cage, counting money.

The *thieves* stuck their guns through the holes in the cage. "This is a *stickup*," one growled. "Open the gate and don't give us any

下一步，麦克吉尼斯和皮诺让整个组织练习抢劫。他们二十多次潜入了大楼，并使用钥匙打开一道又一道的大门。每一次他们都到达了最里面的大门。然后回头离开。

最后，麦克吉尼斯和皮诺决定他们已经做好行动的准备。在1950年1月17日，他们发出了信号。那天晚上，还没到7点，他们各就各位，其中7个人戴上面具钻进了大楼，并打开了5道门。在晚上7:10，他们打开了最里面的门，来到了布林克的办公室。在那里，正如他们预料的，见到了5名警卫，而且都在铁丝网笼子里面，数着现款。

劫匪们把枪伸进笼子的洞里。"打劫！"其中一个咆哮着，"打开门，别制造任何麻烦。"托马斯·罗埃德是警卫队长，看着7支举起来的

innermost *adj.* 最里面的

thief *n.* 小偷

signal *n.* 信号

stickup *n.* 抢劫

trouble." Thomas Lloyd, the head guard, looked at the seven drawn guns. He knew it was hopeless to put up a fight. He *instructed* one of the other guards to go ahead and open the cage door.

Inside the cage, the thieves ordered the guards to lie *facedown* on the floor. They tied the guards' hands behind their backs. In addition, they tied their feet together and put tape across their mouths. Then the crooks grabbed the money. They took all they could carry. In total, they stole more than 1,200 pounds in coins, bills, and checks. By 7:27 p.m. they were out of the building. The robbery had gone perfectly. In cash alone, they had made off with exactly $1,218,211.29!

When news of the heist spread, people were *stunned*. They hadn't thought anyone would ever *dare* rob Brink's. But, clearly, someone

---

枪。他知道打斗是毫无希望的，所以命令其中一名警卫走过去打开笼子的门。

匪徒们来到笼子里面后，命令警卫面朝下趴在地板上。并把警卫的手绑在背后。而且还把他们的脚也绑上，嘴用胶带封好。然后劫匪们开始收集钱款。他们拿走了所有他们能带走的钱。他们总共拿走了重达1200磅的硬币、纸币和支票。到晚上7:27时，他们已经离开了建筑。整个抢劫过程十分完美。光现金他们就拿走了1,218,211.29美元！

当这次抢劫的消息传开之后，人们都被震惊了。他们根本就没有想过居然有人敢抢劫布林克公司。但是的确是有人这么干了。警方根本就没有

---

instruct *v.* 指示　　　　　　　　　　facedown *adv.* 面向下地
stun *v.* 使震惊　　　　　　　　　　dare *v.* 敢；胆敢

had. The police had no clues about who had done it. They *searched* everywhere. They *organized* a huge *manhunt*, but they didn't even know whom they were looking for. All they knew for sure was that the seven robbers were "of medium weight and height."

Meanwhile, the Brink's robbers played it safe. They drove the *loot* to the home of Jazz Maffie in nearby Roxbury. Then each man went back home to his family. The next day they all went to their regular day jobs as if nothing had happened. The thieves stayed calm. They waited a month before splitting up the money. Each man got about $100,000.

For six years, the police tried to solve the crime. They failed. But during that time, trouble was brewing inside the gang. One of the robbers did not like the way the money had been divided. Specs

---

一点罪犯的线索。他们搜查了许多地方。并组织了一次大型的搜捕，但是他们甚至不知道应该找什么人。他们唯一确定的是有7个"中等身材，中等体重"的劫匪。

当时，布林克的劫匪安排得很安全。他们把抢来的东西运到了杰斯·玛菲在罗克斯伯里镇附近的家。然后每个人都回到了自己的家。第二天，他们都回到了日常的工作中，就好像什么都没发生。他们呆得很平静，一个月后在分赃。每个人大约得到10万美元。

6年以来，警方一直在尝试破这个案子。他们没有成功。但是在此期间，这个团伙内部却出现了问题。抢劫者中的一个不喜欢这笔钱的分配方

---

search *v.* 搜索　　　　　　　　　　　organize *v.* 组织
manhunt *n.* 追捕　　　　　　　　　　loot *n.* 掠夺物

O'Keefe began demanding a larger share of the loot. McGinnis and the others became worried. They feared O'Keefe might go to the police. So they *hired* a gunman named Trigger Burke to kill him. One day Burke opened fire as O'Keefe drove by in his car. Luckily for O'Keefe—and unluckily for the rest of the gang—Burke missed his target.

Furious about the attack, O'Keefe did turn to the police. He told them the whole story. The police quickly *rounded up* all the Brink's robbers. The 11 men were brought to trial in 1956. All of them, *including* Specs O'Keefe, were found guilty. Since O'Keefe had helped solve the crime, however, police allowed him to go free. The rest of the gang got long prison terms. In the end, then, the dream of Big Joe McGinnis and Fats Pino had turned into a nightmare.

式。斯伯克斯·奥奇佛要求获得一份更大的份额。麦克吉尼斯和其他的人开始感到忧虑。他们怕奥奇佛到警察那里自首。所以他们雇用了一名叫作特力格·伯克的杀手去杀死他。一天当奥奇佛开车经过时他开枪射击。奥奇佛很幸运，对于团伙的其他人很不幸——伯克没有击中目标。

奥奇佛对这次袭击十分愤怒，他到警方自首了。他说出了他们的整个故事。警方很快抓住了抢劫布林克所有的劫匪。1956年11个人受到审判。包括斯伯克斯·奥奇佛的所有人被判有罪。因为奥奇佛帮助警方侦破了这个案件，他被释放。团伙其他的人被判了很长的刑期。最后大乔麦克吉尼斯和胖子皮诺的梦想变成了噩梦。

---

hire *v.* 雇用
round up 围捕

furious *adj.* 愤怒的
including *prep.* 包括

6

Dumb Criminals

Who's *smarter*—the police or the crooks? If you *judge* by what you see in the movies or on TV, it's the crooks. They always seem to be one step ahead of the cops. The police, on the other hand, are often *portrayed* as bungling fools. In real life, however, it's not like that. In real life, crooks are

This picture could function as an idiot's guide to how to get caught in the act. Real-life stories about the mistakes that criminals make on the job prove that many lawbreakers are not geniuses, to say the least.

蠢贼

这个图片能够简单说明窃贼是怎样被抓住的。罪犯们所犯的真实错误证明了许多窃贼并不是天才。

谁更聪明些——是警察还是窃贼？如果你通过电影或者电视来判断，就是窃贼。看起来他们总是比警察快一步。而警察却总是被描述成笨手笨脚的傻瓜。但是在真实生活中并不是这样。在真实生活中窃贼是周围最蠢的人。下面是他们的一些故事。

smart *adj.* 聪明的
portray *v.* 描绘；扮演

judge *v.* 判断

some of the *dumbest* people around. Here are a few of their stories.

A young man in Flint, Michigan, walked into a gas station wearing a hooded mask. He pulled out a gun and told the clerk to hand over the money. The clerk *obeyed* and the thief quickly ran off with the cash. There was just one problem. The robber was wearing his high school jacket. On it, bold letters spelled out his school, his class year, and his name! By the time the young robber got home, the cops were waiting.

Then there was the case of the car thief in Knox County, Tennessee. When he was brought into court, the judge asked him how he was going to *plead*: guilty or not guilty. It was a *simple* question. But the thief didn't limit his answer to one of those two choices. "Before we go any further, Judge," he said, "let me explain

---

在密歇根的福林特，一个戴着头套的年轻人走进了一家加油站。他举起了手枪让职员把钱递给他。职员服从命令，他迅速地带着钱逃跑了。但是有一个问题。抢劫者穿着他的中学校服。上面用黑体字写着他的学校、年级和姓名！当小窃贼到家时，警察正在等着他。

还有一个盗车贼的故事，那里是田纳西州的克诺克斯县，当他被送上法庭审判时，法官问他如何辩护：有罪还是无罪。这是一个简单的问题。但是窃贼并没有局限于这两个选择。"法官，在我进行下一步之前，"他说，"让我解释一下为什么偷车。"

---

dumb *adj.* 愚蠢的；笨的
plead *v.* 辩护

obey *v.* 服从
simple *adj.* 简单的

why I stole the car."

Many crooks prefer to *strike* at night. They don't want to risk being seen in broad daylight. Also, it's usually easier to get away in the dark. But that was not the case for one thief in Lawrence, Kansas. The man robbed an all-night market at *gunpoint*. After stuffing the loot into his pants, he fled on foot. Local cops rushed to the scene. Two officers saw the man as he ran behind some houses. They *chased* after him, but the crook ran too fast and knew the neighborhood too well. He soon lost the pursuing cops.

The thief felt sure he was safe, but he was wrong. Soon another cop was on his tail. Once more, the thief fled. He *eluded* this third cop, but then a fourth cop appeared. The robber outran one cop after another, but each time a new police officer would take up the

许多窃贼喜欢在晚上发动袭击。他们不想在白天冒着被看到的危险。而且在黑暗中也容易逃跑。但是对于一个肯萨斯州劳伦斯的窃贼来说，却不是这样。他用枪抢劫了一家昼夜服务的商店。把抢来的钱装进裤袋后，他开始步行逃跑。当地的警察都到了这个地方。两个警察见到他在房子中间跑，并追赶起来，但是窃贼跑得很快，而且对这里的地形很熟悉，所以很快就甩掉了后面的警察。

窃贼感到他已经完全安全了，但是他错了。很快另一名警察开始追他。窃贼再次逃跑。他甩掉了第三个警察，但是第四个出现了。他甩掉一个又一个的警察，但是每一次一个新的警察会参加这次接力。窃贼不知道

strike *v.* 攻击；进攻　　　　　gunpoint *n.* 枪口
chase *v.* 追逐；追赶　　　　　elude *v.* 逃避；躲避

chase. The crook couldn't understand how they kept picking up his trail.

At last, the police cornered him. There were simply too many of them. It was only then that the crook discovered his mistake. The *high-tech* sneakers he was wearing had red lights in the heels. Each time he took a step, the lights flashed. So the police had had no trouble at all seeing him in the dark.

Anyone would like to win the *lottery*. But most people who play it lose. Losing is one thing. But losing by one *lousy* number is something else. One Oregon woman couldn't stand the thought that she had almost won. Then she had an idea. What if she took a *ballpoint* pen and changed one wrong number into one right number? Then she would have a winning ticket worth $20.

警察是怎样发现他的逃跑路线的。

最后警察把他包围了。警察太多了。这时窃贼才发现他犯的错误。他穿的高科技跑鞋鞋跟上有红灯。当他迈步时，红灯闪烁。所以警察在黑暗中可以很容易地看到他。

任何人都想赢得彩票。但是大多数的人都会输。输是一回事，而输在一个恶心的号码上是另一回事。有一位俄勒冈的妇女无法拒绝差一点点就赢了的想法。她有了一个主意。如果她用油笔把选错的号码改对怎么样？那样她就能赢得一张价值20美元的彩票。

---

high-tech 高科技
lousy *adj.* 讨厌的；糟糕的

lottery *n.* 彩票
ballpoint *n.* 圆珠笔

The woman just couldn't *resist* the *temptation*. She used her pen to *alter* the number. Then she went to a clerk to cash in the ticket. Unfortunately for her, she wasn't a good *forger*. The clerk saw the change and called the police. As the woman was being taken away, one police officer found out how dumb she really was. He could see the real number under the ink mark. True, it wasn't a $20 winner. It was a $5,000 winner!

Then there was the man who decided to rob a California branch of the Bank of America. On the back of a deposit slip, he wrote a note. It said he was holding up the bank and wanted all the money put in a bag. But as the man waited in line to hand the slip to a teller, he grew nervous. What if someone had seen him writing the note? Maybe someone had already called the cops. The would-be crook

---

这名妇女无法抑止这种诱惑。她用笔改了这个号码，然后到工作人员那里去兑现这张彩票。不幸的是她不是个在行的伪造者。工作人员发现了这变化，然后报了警。当这位妇女被带走时警察发现了她有多么愚蠢。在涂改的墨水下面能够看到原来的号码。当然这就不是赢20美元了，而是赢得了5000美元！

这里还有一个打算抢劫美洲银行加利福尼亚分行的家伙。他在一张存款单的背面写了几句话。上面说：他控制了整个银行，所有的钱都马上装到袋子里。但是就在他排队等候把纸条交给出纳员时，他害怕起来。如果有人看到他写这个纸条怎么办？也许已经有人报警了。这个想象中的罪犯

---

resist *v.* 抵制；抗拒   temptation *n.* 引诱；诱惑
alter *v.* 更改；修改   forger *n.* 伪造者

lost his nerve and walked out of the bank.

He then spied a branch of the Wells Fargo Bank on the other side of the street. Why not rob it instead? So he waited in line at that bank. He handed his note to a Wells Fargo teller. As the teller read it, she saw that it had lots of spelling *errors*. Figuring this *crook* was not very bright, she told him that she could not accept the note because it was written on a Bank of America slip. She said the man would have to write a new stickup note on a Wells Fargo slip. Or he could go back to the Bank of America and use his *original* stickup note there.

The man looked *disappointed*. But he said, "OK." Then he walked out of the bank. Quickly the teller called the police. Officers came and arrested the man as he stood in line at the Bank of America.

害怕了，走出了银行。

　　然后他侦查了旁边的威尔士·法高银行。为什么不抢劫这家？然后在队伍中等待起来。他把纸条递给威尔士·法高的出纳员。出纳员读着纸条，发现上面有许多拼写的错误。她觉得这个劫匪智力不高，就告诉他不能接受这张单据，因为它是用美洲银行的单据写的。他需要用威尔士·法高银行的单据重新写一张。或者回到美洲银行使用他的抢劫单据。

　　看起来这个人很失望。但是他说："好吧。"然后他走出了这家银行。出纳员很快地报了警。警察赶到，在美洲银行排队的队伍里面把那个人逮捕。

---

error *n.* 错误
original *adj.* 原始的；最初的

crook *n.* 骗子；坏蛋
disappointed *adj.* 失望的

One of the dumbest criminals of all time has to be the young man who tried to rob a *grocery* store in San Francisco. Holding a shotgun, the man told the clerk to give him all the cash. The clerk put the money in a bag. But before he could hand it over, the crook spotted a bottle of whiskey on a shelf. Pointing to the bottle, he said, "Put that in the bag too."

The clerk refused. He reminded the robber that the legal drinking age was 21—and he didn't think the robber was that old. The robber *insisted* that he was over 21. The clerk still shook his head. So the robber said, "I'll prove it. Here's my *license*."

The clerk looked at the license and agreed that indeed the robber was old enough to drink. The clerk put the whiskey in the bag along with the money from the *cash register*. After the thief took off with the

---

　　历史上曾经最蠢的罪犯是一个年轻人，他打算抢劫一家位于圣弗朗西斯科的杂货店。他拿着一把猎枪要求营业员把所有的现金都给他。营业员把钱装进袋子里面。但是在他把钱袋递给劫匪之前，劫匪发现了架子上面的一瓶威士忌。他指着瓶子说："把它也装进袋子里面。"

　　营业员拒绝了。他提醒劫匪合法的饮酒年龄是21岁——而且他并不认为劫匪已经够大了。劫匪坚持他已经21岁了。营业员还是摇头。劫匪说："我将证明这一点。这是我的驾驶证。"

　　营业员看了看驾驶证，承认劫匪的确够大，可以饮酒。营业员在交款处把威士忌装进钱袋。当劫匪拿着钱袋离开后，营业员报了警。他把从驾

---

grocery *n.* 食品杂货店
license *n.* 执照；许可证

insist *v.* 坚持；强调
cash register 收银机

bag, the clerk called the police. He gave them the crook's name and address, both of which he had gotten from the driver's license. A few hours later, the cops arrested the crook.

The list of *inept* criminals goes on and on. In one case, a man was charged with stealing money from *vending machines*. He paid his $400 bail with quarters.

Another man ran into a police station shouting, "This is a stickup." He had meant to rob the post office next door.

Then there was the guy who asked a clerk to change a $20 bill. When the clerk opened up the register, the crook *demanded* all the cash. There was only $8 in the *till*. The crook grabbed the money and ran away. He left his $20 behind. And people wonder why the prisons are overcrowded.

驶证上看到的劫匪姓名和地址告诉了警方。几个小时以后，警方逮捕了这个劫匪。

这种不配干罪犯行为的人越来越多。在一起案件中，一个人因为从自动售货机里面偷钱而被捕。并在警察局付出了400美元的保释金。

还有一个人冲进了警察局大喊：“打劫！”他本来打算抢劫旁边的邮局，走错了门。

还有一个人要求店员兑换20美元的零钱。当店员打开收款机时，这个坏蛋要求拿走所有的现金。可收款机里面只有8美元的现金。这个家伙抓起了钱就跑把他自己的20美元落下了。人们总是感到很奇怪为什么监狱人满为患。

---

inept *adj.* 笨拙的；不熟练的

demand *v.* 要求

vending machine 自动售货机

till *n.* （商店、银行的账台中）放钱的抽屉

7

The Real Jesse James

Jesse James is often pictured as a kind of *modern-day* Robin Hood. People talk about how he stole from the rich and gave to the poor. There have been songs, books, and movies about his *heroic* nature. But the real Jesse James was no hero. He was nothing but a thief and a killer.

All of these men appear to be upstanding citizens. However, looks can be deceiving. This is the James gang, a group of notorious bandits and killers in the Old West.

真实的杰西·詹姆斯

所有的这些人看起来好像都是杰出的人士。但是外表是有欺骗性的。这个是詹姆斯匪帮，他们是老西部一伙臭名昭著的土匪和杀人犯。

杰西·詹姆斯经常被描述成现代罗宾汉。人们谈论他是如何劫富济贫的。有大量的歌曲、书籍和电影讲述他的英雄气概。但是真正的杰西·詹姆斯却不是个英雄。他不过是个窃贼和杀人犯。

---

modern-day 现代的；当代的   heroic *adj.* 有英雄气概的

Jesse Woodson James was born near Kearny, Missouri, in 1847. At the age of 15, he went to war. He fought on the side of the South in the Civil War. He was not, however, a regular soldier. Jesse joined a gang of raiders led by the cruel William Quantrill. They attacked and burned the homes of people who sided with the North. When the Civil War ended in 1865, the raiders *broke up*. Jesse and his older brother, Frank, went back to their farms.

No one knows for sure why Jesse and Frank turned to a life of crime. But they did. Maybe, after the thrill of war, farming seemed pretty *dull*. Jesse himself later *blamed* Northerners. He claimed Northerners who had taken over local banks refused to give *loans* to Southern farmers like himself. "We were driven to it," Jesse said. But that was a weak excuse. Jesse James didn't care about the fate of

---

1847年，杰西·伍得逊·詹姆斯出生于密苏里州的科尼镇，15岁时，他去参加了战争。内战中他站在南方一面参战。但是，他并不是一名正规军。杰西加入了由残酷的威廉·奎特力尔率领的一伙兵痞。他们袭击并烧毁那些支持北方军的老百姓住处。到1865年，内战结束时，这伙匪徒分裂了。杰西和他的哥哥佛朗克回到了他们的农场。

没有人确切地知道为什么杰西和佛朗克又回到了罪恶的生涯中。但是他们的确是这样做的。可能在经历了战争的兴奋后，农耕显得很无聊。后来杰西指责北方人。他说占据着当地银行的北方人拒绝给像他这样的南方农民提供贷款。"我们被迫这样做，"杰西说。但这是个虚弱的理由。杰

---

break up （使）（关系）破裂
blame v. 责备

dull adj. 乏味的；无聊的
loan n. 贷款

Southern farmers. After all, most of the people whom he robbed and killed were Southerners. There is no evidence that he ever gave a *dime* of stolen money to the poor—or to anyone else.

Early in 1866, Jesse became a member of an outlaw gang. His brother Frank was in the gang. So were several other old Quantrill raiders. On February 13, 1866, the gang robbed its first bank. The outlaws rode into Liberty, Missouri, in the middle of the day. A few went into the bank. They *threatened* to blow the *bank teller*'s head off unless he gave them all the money.

Meanwhile, the other gang members kept watch outside. After the robbery, the outlaws jumped on their horses and headed out of town. In the street, they passed a college student named George Wymore. He was on his way to class. Seeing the riders *thundering*

西·詹姆斯并不考虑南方农民的命运。毕竟他所抢劫、杀害的大多数人是南方的农民。没有证据表明他给过穷人或者任何人一个硬币。

早在1866年，杰西就成为匪帮的一员。他的哥哥佛朗克也在这个匪帮。里面还有几个其他老奎特力尔匪帮的成员。1866年2月13日，这个匪帮第一次抢劫了银行。在这一天中午，他们骑马闯入密苏里州的自由城。然后进了银行。他们威胁出纳员要么给钱，要么把他们的脑袋打碎。

同时，其他的匪帮成员在外面望风。抢劫之后，匪徒们跳上马，向城外跑去。在街道上，他们遇到了一个叫作乔治·怀莫尔的大学生。他正走在上课的路上。看到这些骑手隆隆地跑过街道，怀莫尔赶紧寻找躲避之

---

dime *n.* 一角硬币
bank teller 银行出纳员

threaten *v.* 威胁
thunder *v.* 发出雷鸣般的响声

down the street, Wymore ran for cover. One of the gang members shot him in the back. He died instantly. It was the first of many times an *innocent* person was gunned down by this gang. Jesse soon showed he was the most daring of the gang members and the most willing to kill. People began to think of him as the gang's leader.

After each bank robbery, Jesse and the rest of the gang went into hiding. They waited for the public outrage to die down. It was usually many months before they hit another bank. Sometimes they passed the time by *ambushing stagecoaches* and robbing the passengers. Then, in 1873, the James gang found a much richer target—trains. That year they planned their first train robbery. They picked the Rock Island Express in Adair, Iowa. Jesse and the other men stopped the train by taking away a piece of the *track*. When engineer John

处。一名匪徒开枪击中了他的后背。他马上就死了。怀莫尔是这个匪帮第一个随手打死的无辜百姓。很快杰西就展示出他是匪徒中胆子最大，最乐意杀戮的人。人们开始把他看作是匪帮的头领。

杰西和同伙们每做一次打劫银行的生意就躲起来一段时间，等待公众的愤怒平息。他们经常要等好几个月才打劫另一家银行。有时他们也抢劫过路的马车和行人来打发时光。在1873年，詹姆斯匪帮发现了一个更为富裕的目标——火车。那一年，他们策划了第一次抢劫火车的行动。他们选择了经过爱何华州阿代尔镇的洛克岛快车。杰西和同伙卸掉了一些铁轨来使火车停下来。当机械师约翰·拉夫里看到被破坏的铁轨时，他马上让

innocent *adj.* 无辜的
stagecoach *n.* 公共马车

ambush *v.* 伏击
track *n.* 轨道

Rafferty saw the broken track, he threw his *engine* into *reverse*. It was too late. The train crashed onto its side, killing Rafferty. James and his gang made off with about $2,000.

By 1874 Jesse James was world famous. He added to his fame with the boldest train robbery up to that time. It took place in the small town of Gad's Hill, Missouri. Not only did Jesse's gang steal all the train's money, but they robbed everyone on board as well. The outlaws loved every minute of it. One grabbed the hat off a passenger's head. Another laughingly told a minister on board to pray for them. Jesse even wrote his own news story about the crime. He left it with a passenger, saying, "Give that to the *editor* of the *St. Louis Dispatch*." Since he hadn't counted the money yet, Jesse left a *blank* space for the amount of money stolen.

发动机倒转。但是太晚了。火车侧翻，拉夫里死亡。詹姆斯和他的匪帮抢劫到2000美元。

到1874年时，杰西·詹姆斯已经世界闻名。当时他所做的最大胆的一次抢劫火车的行动大大加强了他的名气。那是在密苏里的小镇盖德山，杰西匪帮不仅抢劫了列车上所有的现款，也抢劫了所有的乘客。匪徒们十分享受在车上的每一分钟。一个把乘客的礼帽拿掉，还有一个开玩笑地让一名牧师为他们祈祷。杰西甚至自己写了一则新闻报道。把它留给了一名乘客，说："把它交给《圣路易斯新闻》的编辑。"因为当时他还没有数钱，杰西留了一个空格，到时候可以填上丢失的钱数。

---

engine *n.* 引擎；发动机　　　　　　reverse *n.* 倒转
editor *n.* 编辑　　　　　　　　　　blank *adj.* 空白的

Jesse planned each raid carefully. He and his men struck by surprise. Often they met little or no *resistance*. That was because these former Civil War raiders knew how to *terrorize* people. Still, that did not always work. Sometimes the townspeople fought back. One day the gang tried to rob a bank in Savannah, Missouri. Led by a local judge, the citizens drove them away before the outlaws got a nickel. The gang later robbed a bank in Richmond, Missouri. The citizens there formed a posse to chase them. The posse caught three of the robbers and *lynched* them from a nearby tree.

In 1876 the gang was nearly destroyed when the members tried to rob a bank in Northfield, Minnesota. Again they ran into some tough townsfolk. The outlaws tried to scare people by firing shots in the air. They hoped to stir up enough *panic* so they could make a clean

---

杰西的每一次袭击都策划得很仔细。他们经常采用突袭的方式。他们几乎很少遇到抵抗。这是因为这些前内战战士知道如何恐吓。但是这也不总是奏效，有时城镇的居民会回击。一天当匪帮试图抢劫密苏里萨万那镇时，在当地法官的带领下，公民在匪帮抢到一分钱之前把他们赶出城镇。后来匪徒们抢劫了密苏里的里士曼。那里的公民组织了一群人追赶他们，而且抓到了3名匪徒，并在附近的树上私刑处死了他们。

1876年，当匪帮抢劫一家明尼苏达州诺思菲尔德的银行时，几乎完全毁灭。这次他们又进入了强悍的市民当中。匪徒们向空中开枪，试图恐吓他们。他们希望能够激起足够的慌乱，为他们的逃跑扫清道路。但是这

---

resistance *n.* 抵抗；反抗

lynch *v.* 以私刑处死

terrorize *v.* 恐吓；威胁

panic *n.* 恐慌

getaway. But the townspeople knew what the gunshots meant. The bank was being robbed! Several *citizens* sprang into action. They grabbed their guns and took off after the gang. Only Jesse and Frank managed to escape. All the rest of the gang members were *captured* or killed.

Shaken, Jesse and Frank went into hiding. For weeks they dared travel only at night. They slept in barns and stayed alive by eating raw vegetables from the fields. For three years they kept a low profile. They waited for a chance to *resume* their life of crime.

At last, in 1879, Jesse put together a new gang. The robbing and killing began all over again. By this time, many people had had enough of Jesse. The *reward* for his capture or death kept mounting. Lots of people wanted to collect the reward. Jesse knew he had to

些市民知道枪响意味着什么。抢劫银行了！一些市民马上开始行动。他们抓起枪，跟在匪帮的后面。只有杰西和佛朗克逃跑了。其他的匪徒不是被俘就是被杀。

杰西和佛朗克受到很大的震动，他们藏了起来。好几个星期，他们只敢在晚上出来。他们藏在谷仓里，靠吃生的蔬菜活着。在三年里，他们保持着低调。他们等待着时机恢复他们的罪恶生活。

最后，1879年，杰西重新组建了一个新的匪帮。抢劫、杀人重新开始了。到此时，人们已经受够了杰西。俘获或者杀死他的奖金一直在上升。许多人想得到这笔奖励。杰西知道现在他要特别小心。

citizen *n.* 公民；市民
resume *v.* 重新开始；继续

capture *v.* 捕获；俘获
reward *n.* 奖赏

be extra careful now.

Every member of the gang felt the *pressure*. Lawmen might be lurking behind any tree. They might be waiting around any corner. One gang member, Ed Miller, asked Jesse to give up. Jesse *responded* by shooting him. As it turned out, Jesse killed the wrong man. It was gang member Bob Ford who soon turned against Jesse. Ford went to see the *governor* of Missouri. No one ever found out what the governor promised him, but it must have been good. On April 3, 1882, Ford went to see Jesse at his *cabin* near St. Joseph, Missouri. While Jesse's back was turned, Ford pulled out his gun. He shot Jesse James in the back of the head. Some people were saddened by Jesse's death. But others were pleased to see the end of America's most famous outlaw.

匪帮所有成员都感觉到了这种压力。警察可能会躲藏在任何一棵树的后面，可能在任何一个角落里等待着。一名叫作艾得·米勒的匪徒劝杰西投降。杰西用子弹回答了他。后来证明他杀错了人。匪帮成员鲍勃·福特很快就背叛了他，去见了密苏里的州长。没有人知道州长许诺给他什么，但一定很优厚。1882年4月3日，福特到密苏里圣约瑟夫镇杰西的小木屋去看他。当杰西转过身时，福特掏出了枪。一枪击中杰西的后脑。一些人为杰西的死感到悲伤，但是其他人看到美国最著名匪徒的末日都很高兴。

---

pressure *n.* 压力

governor *n.* 州长

respond *v.* 回答；回报

cabin *n.* 小木屋

8

Typhoid Mary

Mary Mallon didn't mean to kill people. For a long time, she didn't even *realize* she was doing it. All she knew was that wherever she went, people got sick. It was a *pattern*. She would be *hired* as a cook by a wealthy New York family. She would begin making meals. But within weeks, the

Confined in a hospital for testing, Mary Mallon glares defiantly at the camera. This seemingly healthy woman never believed what the medical tests revealed— that she was the carrier of typhoid bacteria that killed many people who ate her cooking.

伤寒症玛丽

　　玛丽·麦伦被关在医院里面做检查，她的目光挑衅地对视着镜头。这个看起来健康的妇女根本不相信医学检查出的结果——她是伤寒症病毒的携带者，这种病毒使许多食用了她烹饪食物的人死亡。

　　玛丽·麦伦不想杀人。长期以来她甚至没有意识到她正在做着这件事。她所知道的只是无论她到哪里，人们都会生病。这是一个规律。曾有一个富裕的纽约家庭雇用她做厨师。并开始做饭。但是几个星期之内，这个家庭就会得上一种叫作"伤寒"的可怕疾病。

realize *v.* 认清；认识到　　　　　　　　　　　pattern *n.* 模式；方式
hire *v.* 雇用

family would come down with a *horrible* disease called *typhoid*.

The disease began with chills and a fever. Victims often felt sick to their stomach. They developed a headache and suffered from *nosebleeds*. Next, they broke out with a bright red rash. They began coughing. Sometimes the fever would break and they would recover. In other cases, their condition would worsen and they would die.

In the early 1900s few people understood how typhoid is spread. Some people thought it came from *spoiled* milk. Others thought it came from garbage fumes. Only a few scientists had figured out the truth: it is caused by germs that live inside the human body. These germs pass through the body when a person uses the toilet. Sometimes the germs get on a person's hands. If the person touches food before washing up, the germs can be transferred to the food.

这种疾病开始时发冷，发烧。受害者经常感到肚子痛。头痛和鼻子出血。然后会出现鲜红色的皮疹，并且开始咳嗽。有时发热会停止，他们就痊愈了。但是另一些人会变糟，直到死亡。

在20世纪早期，几乎没有人知道伤寒症是怎样传播的。一些人认为是放坏了的牛奶产生的。另一些人认为是垃圾的臭气产生的。只有一些科学家找到了事实的真相：它是由人体内的细菌产生的。当人排泄时这些细菌会出来。有时，细菌会传播到人的手上。如果人没有洗手就接触食物，细菌就会传播到食物上。任何食用这些食物的人都会感染上细菌。在20世

---

horrible *adj.* 可怕的
nosebleed *n.* 鼻出血

typhoid *n.* 伤寒（病）
spoiled *adj.* （食物）变质的

Anyone who eats the food can then come down with the disease. In the early 1900s, about one out of every five people sick with typhoid died.

Mary Mallon had never had typhoid. She had always been healthy and strong. She had no reason to think she might be passing the disease on to anyone. And yet... no matter where she went, typhoid soon followed. Mary's *reaction* to this problem was simple. She ran away. Once she did stay and help nurse a family through the *illness*. But the rest of the time, she just packed her bags and *moved on*.

In 1906 Mary got a job as the cook for Charles Warren and his family. She had been with the Warrens just three weeks when one of the children got a fever. Mary knew what that meant. Typhoid had struck again. Quickly she *collected* her pay. Then she took off.

纪早期患伤寒症的五个人中有一个人死亡。

玛丽·麦伦从没有得过伤寒症，而且总是健康强壮。没有理由相信她可能会把疾病传染给别人。但是，无论她到哪里，伤寒症都会跟到哪里。玛丽对于此问题的反应很简单。她会逃跑。一次她的确留了下来，帮助照料这个家庭。但是其余的时候她都会打包然后搬走。

1906年玛丽得到一份工作，作为查尔斯·沃伦家的厨师。她在沃伦家刚刚待了三个星期，一个孩子就发烧了。玛丽知道这意味着什么。伤寒症又开始了。她很快要回了工资，然后就离开了。但是这一次玛丽被追踪

---

reaction n. 反应　　　　　　　illness n. 病；疾病
move on 离开　　　　　　　　collect v. 取；领取

But this time she was followed. A man named George Soper began *investigating* the Warren family's illness.

Soper was an expert on diseases. He knew how typhoid was spread. He figured that healthy people could carry typhoid germs around without knowing it. Perhaps, he thought, Mary Mallon was a carrier of these germs. He decided to track her down. He wanted to run tests to see if her body housed typhoid germs.

Soper found Mary in March of 1907. She was working as a cook for yet another New York family. As Soper had feared, a girl in the house was already dying of typhoid. Soper went to the house. Mary was in the kitchen. When Soper told her why he had come, she became *furious*. She picked up a huge carving *fork* and *lunged* at him. Soper managed to run away without being hurt.

了。一个叫作乔治·索普尔的人开始调查沃伦家族的疾病。

索普尔是研究疾病方面的专家。他知道伤寒症是如何传播的。他考虑到健康的人也可能会在不知情的情况下携带伤寒病毒，而且认为也许玛丽·麦伦就是这种病毒的携带者，就决定跟踪她。他想用试验来检验她的体内是否藏匿了伤寒病毒。

索普尔在1907年3月发现了玛丽。她正为另一个纽约家庭做厨师工作。正如索普尔所担心的，这一家的小女孩已经奄奄一息了。索普尔到了这个家庭。玛丽正在厨房。当索普尔告诉她来意后，玛丽勃然大怒。她抓起了一把雕刻用的大叉子向他刺去。索普尔成功逃跑，没有受伤。

---

investigate *v.* 调查
fork *n.* 叉；餐叉

furious *adj.* 暴怒的
lunge *v.* 冲；扑

Soon after that, Soper went to see where Mary lived. It was a dirty, smelly place. Standing in the filth, Soper understood how Mary could spread typhoid to so many people. She clearly had very poor health habits.

Soper sent Dr. Josephine Baker to talk to Mary. Baker worked for the city. It was her job to protect people from health *hazards*. But Baker had no luck, either. Mary simply did not believe what the doctor told her. It sounded crazy. After all, she was healthy. Surely she was not carrying typhoid around inside her body. Mary just wanted everyone to leave her alone. She wanted to go on earning a living as a cook. And as for washing her hands after using the toilet—well, that seemed like a waste of time and *energy*.

Baker and other city *officials* did not know what to do. At last

---

没过多长时间，索普尔去看玛丽的住处。那是一个肮脏、充满臭气的地方。站在这样一个肮脏的地方索普尔知道了为什么玛丽能够把伤寒症传播给那么多的人。很明显她的卫生习惯很糟糕。

索普尔让约瑟芬·贝克尔博士去和玛丽谈。贝克尔为整个城市工作，任务是保护市民免受疾病的灾难。但是贝克尔也是运气不佳。玛丽就是不相信博士告诉她的情况。听起来好像发疯了，毕竟她的身体健康。的确她的身体没有感染伤寒症病毒。玛丽只是想一个人待着，想做厨师谋生。至于上完厕所洗手，在她看来完全是浪费时间和精力。

贝克尔和其他的城市官员不知道应该怎么做。最后他们决定把她锁

---

hazard *n.* 危险；有危险的事物　　　　energy *n.* 精力；活力
official *n.* 官员

they decided to lock Mary up. It was a *desperate* move. But no one could think of any other way to stop her from spreading typhoid. Baker and five police officers went to get her. When Mary saw them coming, she fled. After a two-hour search, she was found *crouching* in a neighbor's yard. When the police grabbed her, she began kicking and biting. It took all five officers to drag her into an *ambulance*. Said Dr. Baker, "I literally sat on her all the way to the hospital. It was like being in a cage with an angry lion."

Mary was kept at the hospital for months. As expected, tests showed that her body was full of typhoid germs. That fall, she was *transferred* to a hospital on a tiny island near the city. She was kept there for three years. She got a lawyer to help her fight for her freedom. She argued that it was illegal for the city to hold her

---

起来。这是个没有办法的办法。但是没有人想出另一个阻止她传播伤寒病菌的方法。贝克尔和5名警察去逮捕她。当玛丽看到他们到来时，便逃跑了。在两个小时的搜索后，在邻居家的庭院里面找到了她。当警察抓住她时她开始又踢又咬。所有5名警察一起上，才把她拖上了救护车。贝克尔博士说："可以说在去往医院的路上，我是坐在她的身上。就好像是同一头愤怒的狮子关在一起。"

　　玛丽被关在医院里面几个月。正如所预料的那样，检查表明她的身体充满了伤寒病菌。那一年的秋天，她被送到城市附近一座小岛上的一个医院。她被关在那里3年。她请了一名律师为她的自由而战。她争论说城市

---

desperate *adj.* 绝望的
ambulance *n.* 救护车

crouch *v.* 蹲伏；蜷缩
transfer *v.* 转移

prisoner. Mary was right, but no judge was willing to set her free. And so she remained locked up on North Brother Island.

In 1910 Mary finally agreed to do what the doctors wanted. If they let her go, she said, she would never work as a cook again. She also promised to check in with them every three months. Doctors agreed to the plan. They turned Mary loose. But as soon as she was back on the streets, she *vanished*. For five years, no city official could find her.

During that time, Mary *floated* from one restaurant job to the next. She cooked for hotels. She cooked in diners. She made up different names for herself. And she *ran away* whenever one of her customers got typhoid.

In 1915 Mary got a kitchen job at the Sloane Hospital for Women

---

把她关起来是违法的。玛丽是对的，但是没有法官愿意把她放出来。所以她一直被锁在北方兄弟岛上。

在1910年，玛丽同意医生们所说的。并且说如果他们让自己走，她将再也不做厨师，还同意每3个月回来检查一次。医生们同意这个计划，放松了对她的管制。但是她一回到街上，就消失了。整整5年，城市的官员都没有找到她。

在那段时间，玛丽从一个饭馆的工作游荡到另一个。她为旅店、小饭店烹调，她自己编造了一些名字。如果她的一个顾客得了伤寒症，她就会逃跑。

1915年，玛丽在斯龙恩纽约市女子医院找到了一个厨师的工作。很

---

vanish *v.* 突然完全消失   float *v.* 漂泊；飘荡
run away 逃跑

in New York City. Soon 25 people there came down with typhoid. One of the workers joked that the cook must be the *infamous* Typhoid Mary. Terrified of being caught again, Mary took off for New Jersey. But now police were on her trail. On May 27, 1915, she was arrested and returned to North Brother Island.

Mary Mallon had reached the end of the line. Health officials were not going to give her any more chances. They decided to keep her on that little island for the rest of her life. For 22 years, until her death at age 70, that's where Mary stayed. In her later years, she was given her own *cottage* to live in. She could have visitors whenever she wanted. At mealtime, though, everyone knew what to do. They always left without eating a bite of Typhoid Mary's cooking.

快那里的25个人得了伤寒。其中一名工作人员开玩笑道，他们的厨师一定是声名狼藉的"伤寒症玛丽"。玛丽害怕再被抓住，便出发前往新泽西。但是现在警察已经在路上等待她了。1915年5月27日，玛丽被逮捕，被送回到北方兄弟岛。

玛丽·麦伦已经触到了界线。健康官员不再给她任何机会。他们决定让她在那个小岛上度过余生。直到她70岁去世，整整22年她都一直待在那里。在她最后的几年，她得到了一个自己使用的小房子。只要她想见参观者，就能见到。但是在用餐时所有的人都知道怎么做。他们经常一点也不品尝伤寒症玛丽烹调的食品就溜走了。

infamous *adj.* 声名狼藉的　　　　　　　　　cottage *n.* 小屋

How Bad Was Ma Barker?

Was she "Bloody Mama"? Or was she just plain Mom? Was she the brains who planned all the bank robberies and murders? Or was she just a *doting* mother who never thought her sons did anything wrong? If you believe the movies and the *FBI*, Kate "Ma" Barker was bad, really bad. But if you believe

The FBI believed Ma Barker was the brains behind an unusual family business—robbing, murdering, and kidnapping. Some of the gang's weapons are shown here on the porch of the family hideout.

贝克尔大妈

　　联邦调查局相信，贝克尔大妈是一个非同寻常的家族产业背后的策划者——抢劫、谋杀和绑架。这里在他们家族窝点的门廊上展示了这个匪帮的一部分武器。

　　她是"残忍的大妈"吗？或者她就是普通的大娘？她是所有银行抢劫和谋杀案的策划者吗？或者她只是一个溺爱孩子的母亲，从来不认为她的孩子们会干错事？如果你相信电影和联邦调查局，大妈凯特·贝克尔是坏蛋，彻底的坏蛋。但是如果你相信这个帮会的成员，"这位老妇女甚至不能准备早餐。"

doting *adj.* 溺爱的；宠爱的　　　　　　　　　　FBI *abbr.* 联邦调查局

the gang members, "The old woman couldn't plan breakfast."

Kate was still a teenager when she married George Barker in 1892. He was a poor farmer with no *ambition*. It was not a happy marriage. Still, the Barkers had four boys—Herman, Lloyd, Doc, and Freddie. The Barkers moved around a lot, living in one tarpaper shack after another. George was almost worthless as a father. When his rowdy boys got into trouble with his neighbors, he shrugged. "You'll have to talk to Mother," he would say. "She *handles* the boys."

Ma Barker had a different response to the neighbors. When they accused her sons of some *prank*, she lashed out. She screamed and called them *liars*. Her sons were innocent—always.

As the Barker brothers grew older they moved up the ladder of crime. At first they were petty thieves. When the cops arrested them,

---

1892年，当凯特还只十几岁时，就与乔治·贝克尔结婚了。他是一个毫无抱负的农夫。这是一个不幸福的婚姻。可是，贝克尔一家还是有4个男孩——赫尔曼、罗埃德、多克和弗里第。这一家经常迁移，居住在一个又一个的油毡纸棚子里面。作为父亲来讲，乔治几乎是无用的。当他的如同小流氓一样的孩子们与邻居发生麻烦时，他只是耸耸肩膀说："你得和他们妈妈谈，她处理孩子的问题。"

贝克尔大妈对待邻居有完全不同的反应。当邻居们指责贝克尔的孩子胡闹时，她经常猛烈地与他们争吵，尖叫着把他们叫作骗子，而她的儿子们总是无辜的。

随着贝克尔兄弟的成长，犯罪的行动也在升级。刚开始他们是一些小

---

ambition *n.* 抱负；志向
prank *n.* 恶作剧；胡闹

handle *v.* 处理；应付
liar *n.* 说谎的人

Ma came to the rescue. She cried, begged, and pleaded with the police to let her boys go. Many times, that's what they did.

In the late 1910s the boys began robbing banks. The FBI said Ma Barker planned the robberies. They said she told the boys what to do. She even checked out all the *getaway* routes. She knew how long it would take to escape on this road or that road. She knew how much more time would be needed if it rained. According to the FBI, Ma ruled her boys with an iron fist. Although she never robbed any banks in person, she was the *brilliant* mind behind all the crimes.

That is one *version* of Ma Barker.

The other version comes from members of the gang. The Barker brothers often *joined up* with other hoods. One was Alvin "Creepy" Karpis. He said Ma didn't do a thing. The gang planned everything

---

贼。当警察逮捕他们时，妈妈就来营救。她哭喊着，乞求着，祷告着要求警察让她的孩子们回家。有许多次这样的情况，可见他们都做了些什么。

在20世纪前十年的后期，孩子们开始抢劫银行。联邦调查局说是贝克尔大妈策划了这些行动，是她告诉孩子们去干什么，甚至检查了逃跑的路线。她知道在这条路上逃跑和那条路上逃跑所用的时间，也知道如果下雨需增加多少时间。按照联邦调查局的说法，大妈是用铁腕来统治她的男孩们。虽然她从未直接参与抢劫银行的行动，但她是藏在案子后面的黑手。

这是关于贝克尔大妈的一个版本。

另一个版本来自于团伙内部。贝克尔兄弟经常和一些其他的流氓混在一起。一个叫作"麻烦"的艾尔文·卡皮斯说大妈没有做任何事情。团伙

---

getaway *adj.* 逃跑用的
version *n.* 版本

brilliant *adj.* 有才能的
join up 联合起来

when she wasn't around. "It's no insult to Ma's memory," Karpis later wrote, "that she just didn't have the brains or know-how to *direct* us. We'd leave her at home when we were *arranging* a job, or we'd send her to a movie. Ma saw a lot of movies."

While people argue about Ma Barker's true role, no one disputes what her boys did. They conducted their own personal crime wave. They robbed banks and trains. In time, they added murder and kidnapping to their list of *felonies*.

One by one, the sons paid for their crimes. Lloyd was tried and found guilty of mail robbery. The judge gave him 25 years in prison. (When he got out of prison, Lloyd gave up his life of crime. He served in the Army during World War II. Even so, he came to a *violent* end. His wife shot and killed him in 1949.)

在她不在的时候才进行策划。"这并不是对大妈印象的污辱，"卡皮斯后来写道，"她根本就没有头脑来指挥我们。我们策划一次工作时要把她留在家里，或者给她安排一次电影。大妈看过许多场电影。"

虽然人们对贝克尔大妈真实的角色有争论，但是对于她孩子的所作所为是确定无疑的。他们做了大量的罪恶行径。他们抢劫银行和列车，有时还在他们的重罪单上加上谋杀和绑架。

她的儿子们一次又一次地为他们的罪恶付出代价。罗埃德因抢劫邮政部门被判有罪。法官判他服刑25年。（他出狱后，就结束了犯罪的生涯。参军并参加了二战。即使是这样，他也是暴亡，1949年他的妻子枪杀了他。）

---

direct *v.* 管理；控制
felony *n.* 重罪

arrange *v.* 安排
violent *adj.* 暴力的

Herman also died a violent death. On August 1, 1927, he shot and killed a police officer after robbing a bank. Four weeks later, Ma's boy shot another cop. He and two other gang members had just robbed a store. In the gun battle with police, Herman was shot but not killed. Seeing no way out, he turned his gun on himself and took his own life. According to the FBI, Herman's death turned Ma Barker into a "beast of prey." In her *grief*, she ruled the gang with even *harsher authority*.

If Ma did indeed become heartless, that would have been just fine with Doc. He was the most *ruthless* of all the brothers. Once, when the gang wanted one of its own members killed, Doc quickly volunteered. He shot the man in a barn. Then he soaked everything in gasoline and set the barn on fire. Later Doc bragged about the

---

赫尔曼也是暴亡。1927年8月1日，他在抢劫银行时，枪杀了一名警察。4周后大妈的孩子又枪杀了一名警察。和另外两名团伙成员去抢劫商店，与警察的枪战中赫尔曼被射中，但是没有死。可是他发现已经没有突围的可能就饮弹自尽了。按照联邦调查局的说法，赫尔曼的死使贝克尔大妈转向了"牺牲者的胸膛"。她在悲哀之中，使用更加严厉的权威来统治这个帮会。

如果大妈的确变得冷酷无情，可能对多克会好一点。他是他们兄弟中最肆无忌惮的。一次他们帮会要杀死一个内部成员，多克很快就自愿出发了，并把那个人击毙在一个谷仓里，然后在里面浇上汽油，将谷仓烧毁。

---

grief *n.* 悲痛
authority *n.* 权力；权威

harsh *adj.* 严厉的；严酷的
ruthless *adj.* 无情的；残忍

killing. In a note he wrote to some of the other gang members, he said, "I took care of that business for you boys. It was done just as good as if you did it yourself. Always at your service. Ha, ha!"

In 1922 Doc was *convicted* for killing a night watchman during one of the gang's robberies. The court sentenced him to life in prison. He was later given a *pardon*. The governor of Oklahoma told him to get out of the state and never come back. But Doc couldn't *stay out of* trouble. Soon he was back in prison. On January 13, 1939, Doc tried to escape. The guards saw him and opened fire. Badly wounded, Doc was taken back to prison. He died the next day.

By 1935 Ma and Freddie were the only Barkers still free. That was about to end. Ma and her youngest son were hiding out in Florida. The FBI was after them for kidnapping. A tip led *federal* agents to a

---

后来多克对这次谋杀大肆吹嘘。后来在他写给另一个团伙成员的纸条上，说："我为你们干了那次生意。干得像你自己做得那么干净。永远为你服务。哈，哈！"

1922年，多克又在团伙的一次抢劫中杀害了一个夜间看守。法庭宣判他终身监禁。后来虽然获得了赦免，但俄克拉荷马州的州长命令他离开这个州，永远不许回来。但多克还是惹麻烦，很快又入狱了。1939年1月13日，多克试图逃跑。警卫看到了他并开火。多克身受重伤，被抓回了监狱，第二天就死了。

1935年，大妈和弗里第是贝克尔家族仅剩下自由的幸存者。这一切快要结束了。大妈和他最小的儿子藏在佛罗里达。联邦调查局为了一桩绑

---

convict *v.* 宣判……有罪　　　　　　　　　　pardon *n.* 赦免
stay out of 置身于……外　　　　　　　　　　federal *adj.* 联邦的

cottage at Lake Weir. Early on January 16, agents surrounded the cottage. They called for the Barkers to *toss out* their guns and come out with their hands up. Freddie gave his answer with a burst of machine gun fire.

The *ensuing* battle lasted for four hours. Each side fired away for about 15 minutes. Then there was a period of silence. That was followed by another round of gunfire. "It was like war," said a woman who lived across from the Barkers. "I was suddenly *awakened* by guns firing. I got out of bed, and as I stood up some bullets came through the closed door." The woman and her daughter climbed out a back window and ran for safer ground.

At last, around 11 A.M., the firing stopped for good. One man went into the house to check out the scene. He soon *reappeared*.

架罪而跟踪他们。一条线索把联邦调查局的特工们引到了维尔湖边的小屋。在1月16日凌晨,特工们包围了这个小屋,并让贝克尔一家把枪扔出来,并把手举过头顶。弗里第用一连串的机枪射击回答了他们。

随之而来的战斗大约进行了4个小时。双方大约各射击了15分钟。然后是一阵寂静,然后又是一阵交火。"就像是战争一样,"一名居住在贝克尔对面的女士说。"我被突然的开火声惊醒。我起了床,刚刚站起来,一些子弹就打穿了大门。"这位女士和她的女儿从后窗爬了出去,跑到更安全的地方。

最后在上午11点,枪击结束了。一个特工进入房间检查。不一会,他又出现了。"他们都死了,"特工说。

---

toss out 扔出
awaken *v.* 唤醒;激起

ensuing *adj.* 接着发生的
reappear *v.* 再次出现

67

"They are all dead," he said.

Freddie had been shot more than a dozen times. Ma Barker had just one bullet in her. The agents reported that she went down with "a machine gun in her hands". But was she shot by an agent's bullet or did she kill herself? Some people think that she shot herself in despair after Freddie died. No one knows for sure.

With her death, the FBI turned Ma Barker into a *legend*. As far as the world was *concerned*, she was "Bloody Mama". Many people called her Public Enemy Number One. Hollywood shared this view. A movie about her life shows her being shot with a blazing machine gun in her hands. But was she really an outlaw or just the mother of outlaws? Today many experts have their doubts. They think the gang members were telling the truth when they said Ma Barker was *clueless*. They think that perhaps Kate Barker was just a mom — a bad mom — but still just a mom.

弗里第身上的枪伤超过12个。贝克尔大妈身上只有一枪。特工们报告说她"手持机关枪"倒地。但是她是被特工打死的呢还是自杀？一些人认为她看到弗里第死后自杀了。没有人知道确切的结论。

随着她的死去，联邦调查局把贝克尔大妈变成了一个传奇。如世人所知，她是"凶残的大妈"。许多人称她"第一号人民公敌"。好莱坞也同意这个观点。一个关于她一生的电影展示出她在用机枪开火时被击毙。但是她是一个真正的匪徒还是只是匪徒的妈妈？今天许多专家存有疑点。他们认为帮会成员说大妈是无辜的这一点是真的。他们认为也许凯特·贝克尔就是妈妈——一个坏妈妈——但仍旧是妈妈。

---

legend n. 传奇
clueless adj. 愚笨的；无能的

concerned adj. 关心的；担心的

10

Dillinger: A Crook with Style

John Dillinger could have done anything he wanted with his life. He was a smart kid with a lot of friends. He had *plenty of courage*. And he was a *terrific athlete*. In fact, the governor of Indiana once declared, "That kid ought to be playing major league baseball." But John Dillinger did not become a baseball player or a

Even crooks need a break now and then. John Dillinger thought so when he took a girlfriend to the movies at this theater in Chicago. He didn't know she had tipped off FBI agents, who waited for him outside.

第林格：有风度的坏蛋

即使是坏人有时也需要休息。约翰·第林格也这样认为，他带着他的女朋友去芝加哥的剧场看电影。他并不知道他的女朋友已经告诉了联邦调查局的特工。他们正在门口等着他。

约翰·第林格一生中为所欲为。他是一个有许多朋友的小孩。而且有足够的勇气。他是个极好的运动员。实际上，印第安纳州的州长曾经宣称，"那个孩子应该去打垒球。"但是约翰·第林格没有成为垒球运动员，或者商人、教师。他成了一名罪犯。

---

plenty of 大量；许多
terrific *adj.* 极好的

courage *n.* 勇气；胆量
athlete *n.* 运动员

businessman or a teacher. He became a criminal.

Dillinger was born in *Indianapolis*, Indiana, in 1903. By the time he got to sixth grade, he was already breaking the law. He stole coal from a railroad yard. Then he sold it to neighbors as heating fuel for their homes.

Dillinger got into real trouble when he was 21. He tried to rob an elderly store owner. No one was hurt in the robbery, but Dillinger wound up in police hands. The police *encouraged* him to plead guilty. They *assured* him that if he did, the judge would go easy on him. Dillinger took their advice and pleaded guilty. But the judge was in a bad mood that day. He slapped Dillinger with a sentence of 10 to 20 years.

The harsh *punishment* shocked everyone. The store owner himself later asked that the sentence be cut down. Even so, Dillinger served

---

1903年第林格出生于印第安纳州的印第安纳波利斯。当上到六年级时，他就已经开始犯罪了。他从铁路煤厂里面偷煤炭，然后卖给邻居作为燃料。

21岁时，他真的遇到了麻烦。他试图抢劫一名年老的店主。这次抢劫中没有人受伤，但是第林格被警察抓住了。警察让他承认有罪，并告诉说如果他承认，法官不会过于追究的。第林格接受了他们的建议，承认有罪。但是那一天法官的情绪不好，判处第林格10至20年的刑期。

这个严厉的判处震惊了每个人。后来店主自己也请求减轻刑期。即使

Indianapolis *n.* 印第安纳波利斯
assure *v.* 保证；担保

encourage *v.* 鼓励
punishment *n.* 惩罚

nine years in prison. By the time he got out, he was filled with *contempt* for the law. Still, from his point of view, the years in prison had not been a total loss. He had become friends with some other *convicts*. They had taught him everything they knew about robbing banks. When Dillinger was released, he promised not to forget them. He vowed to return and help them escape as soon as he could.

First, though, Dillinger needed some cash. So, in the summer of 1933, he robbed a string of banks. Dillinger planned his crimes with great care. He studied the alarm *system* of each bank. He laid out escape routes and picked good *hideouts*. But what really set Dillinger apart from other robbers was the style he brought to the job. He would stroll into a bank dressed in a nice suit. Pulling out his gun, he would politely ask the tellers to hand over the money. Often he would leap over a railing or two, moving with an easy grace that

---

是这样，第林格还是在监狱里面待了9年。当他出狱时，心中充满了对法律的不满。可是按照他的观点，在监狱的时光并非完全是浪费。第林格与许多罪犯成了朋友。他们教给他所有抢劫银行的方法。当被释放时，他许诺不会忘记他们，并发誓会回来帮助他们逃跑。

首先，第林格需要一些现金。所以在1933年的夏季，他抢劫了一系列的银行。第林格极其小心地策划了行动。他研究了银行的报警系统，画出了逃跑路线，选择了很好的躲避地点。但是真正把第林格与其他窃贼区分开的，是他干活的方式。他会穿着一身上好的西装，踱步进入银行，然后掏出枪礼貌地请出纳交出钱。他可能也会跳过一个或两个栏杆，优雅的

---

contempt *n.* 轻视；蔑视
system *n.* 系；系统

convict *n.* 罪犯
hideout *n.* 隐匿处

impressed everyone. Sometimes he would even flirt with women in the bank. Word of his actions spread quickly. More and more people began to talk about this *dashing* bank robber named John Dillinger.

By September Dillinger had quite a stash of money. True to his word, he remembered his friends back in prison. He arranged to have weapons smuggled in to them. Armed with those *weapons*, 10 of Dillinger's buddies broke free.

Over the next 12 months, Dillinger and this gang of thieves tore across the country. They robbed bank after bank. Sometimes they got just a few thousand dollars. But often they made off with much more. On October 23, 1933, they walked away with more than $75,000. It was Dillinger's biggest *haul*. It was also the robbery that made him a folk hero in the eyes of many people. Again, it wasn't just what he did—it was the way he did it.

动作打动了每一个人。有时第林格甚至会同银行里面的女子调情。关于他行为的传言散布得很快。越来越多的人开始谈论一个叫作约翰·第林格的潇洒抢劫犯。

在9月，第林格有了一大笔钱。他坚持着他的诺言，还想着狱中的朋友们，安排给他们偷运武器。第林格的10个好朋友用这些武器逃出了监狱。

在其后的12个月里，第林格和他的团伙横扫整个美国。他一家接一家地抢劫银行。有时他们只得到几千美元，但是经常能弄到更多的钱。在1933年10月23日，他们带着七万五千多美元离开了。这次是第林格最大的一次收获。也是这次抢劫使他在许多人的心中成为民间英雄。同样，这次不是他做了什么——而是他做的方式。

---

impress *v.* 给予某人深刻印象   dashing *adj.* 潇洒的
weapon *n.* 武器；兵器   haul *n.* 赃物；非法物品

On that October day, Dillinger and his men went to Greencastle, Indiana. They entered the Central National Bank. With a gun in his hand, Dillinger made a *dramatic leap* over a railing. He and his men then stuffed *fistfuls* of money into their sacks. As they were leaving, Dillinger noticed a man off to the side. He was a farmer who had come to put some money in the bank. His money still lay on the counter in front of a teller's window.

Dillinger looked at the stack of bills. "Is that your money or the bank's?" he asked.

"Mine," said the farmer.

"Keep it," Dillinger told him. "We only want the bank's."

It was that kind of remark that made Dillinger famous. Sure, he was a crook, people said. But he was such an *honorable* crook! The police took a different view. They knew Dillinger and his gang had

---

在10月1日，第林格和他的人来到印第安纳的格林喀斯特尔，他们进入了中央国家银行。第林格手持枪支，令人惊奇地跳过了栏杆。他和他的人大把大把地把钱装进袋子里。当他们离开时，第林格注意到旁边的一个人。他是一个农夫，来存钱，并且钱还放在出纳员前面的柜台上。

第林格看看这堆钱。问道："这是你的钱还是银行的？"

"我的，"农夫说。

"拿好，"第林格告诉他，"我们只拿银行的。"

就是这个说法使第林格闻名。当然他是个坏蛋，但是是这样一个可敬的坏蛋！警察有不同的看法。他们知道第林格和他的团伙杀了几个人。他

---

dramatic *adj.* 引人注目的
fistful *n.* 一把

leap *n.* 跳跃；飞跃
honorable *adj.* 可敬的

killed several people. The thieves shot anyone who got in their way. More *victims* could fall any day. So the FBI put Dillinger on their Most Wanted list.

Actually, the police got their hands on Dillinger a couple of times. But both times he broke out of jail before a trial could be held. His most *spectacular* escape came on March 3, 1934. Dillinger had been put in jail in Crown Point, Indiana. Everyone said that jail was escape-proof. Dozens of extra guards were brought in just to make sure of that. Somehow, though, John Dillinger got his hands on a weapon. It is not clear whether he used a real gun or simply a piece of wood shaped like a gun. In any case, it looked real enough to the guards. Dillinger flashed it at them, then escaped down a flight of stairs.

By July 1934 Dillinger's gang had stolen more than $250,000.

们会向任何一个拦路人开火。某一天可能会有更多的受害者倒下。所以联邦调查局把第林格列在"通缉要犯"的名单中。

实际上，警方抓住过他两次，但是每一次他都成功地在审判前越狱了。他最特别的一次逃脱是在1934年3月3日。第林格被送到印第安纳的科隆波特。每个人都说在那个监狱是不可能跑掉的。还调用了几十个额外的警卫来保证。但是约翰·第林格却操起了一支枪。还不知道这是一支真枪，还是一支像枪的木棍。无论怎样，警卫们看起来是足够真了。第林格指着他们，然后逃下了楼梯。

到1934年7月为止，第林格的团伙已经窃得250,000美元。而且他们只是在几个月之内就取得了这些。但是第林格作为一个高高飞在天上的匪

---

victim *n.* 受害者；牺牲者　　　　　　spectacular *adj.* 引人注目的

And they had done it in just a few months. But Dillinger's days as a high-flying gangster were coming to an end. According to police, he was *betrayed* by one of his girlfriends. Anna Sage came to the Chicago police. She offered to take them to Dillinger. In return, they agreed to help her get out of some legal troubles.

Police records show that on July 22, Sage went to a movie with Dillinger. She wore a red dress so police agents could spot her in the crowd. When she walked out of the theater with Dillinger, six agents moved in. *Sensing* trouble, Dillinger *whirled* and reached for his gun. But the agents were ready. Three of them fired at Dillinger, who dropped to the ground, dead.

That is one version of the story. But another version says that it was not John Dillinger who died outside a Chicago theater that day. According to this story, Anna Sage *tricked* police. She had told them

---

徒的日子却到了尽头。按照警方的说法，他被他的一个女朋友出卖了。安娜·赛奇来到了芝加哥的警察局，说能够找到第林格。作为报答，他们同意帮助她摆脱一些法律麻烦。

警察记录显示在7月22日，赛奇和第林格去看电影。她穿着红色的裙子，这样警察在人群中能够找到她。当她和第林格一起从剧场出来时，6名特工跟了上去。第林格觉得有问题，他转过身，掏枪。但是特工们已经准备好了，3名特工向他开枪，他倒在地上，死了。

那是这个故事的一个版本。但是另一个版本说，那天在芝加哥剧场前倒地的不是约翰·第林格。按照这种说法，安娜·赛奇欺骗了警方，说

---

betray v. 出卖；背叛
whirl v. 转；旋转

sense v. 感觉到
trick v. 欺骗

that she would be with Dillinger. However, some people claim, her unfortunate *companion* was really a *small-time* crook named Jimmy Lawrence.

There are a few facts to support this *theory*. Doctors who examined the body said the dead man had a damaged heart. Dillinger could not have made his fancy leaps with such a heart. He could never have played baseball, either. Doctors said they found no *scars* on the dead man. But Dillinger's body should have shown a couple of old bullet wounds. Finally, doctors said the dead man's eyes were brown. Dillinger's were blue.

It may be that the doctors were sloppy when they examined Dillinger's body. Or it may be that police shot the wrong man. We'll never know for sure. All we know is this: after July 22, 1934, John Dillinger never bothered anyone again.

她和第林格一起走。然而，有人声称，她不幸的同伴是一个小有名气的恶棍，叫作吉米·劳伦斯。

有几个事实可以支持这种说法。检查了尸体的医生说死去的家伙的心脏受过伤。第林格能够做那样惊险的跳跃动作，不可能有这样的心脏。死去的家伙也不可能玩过垒球。医生说他们在尸体上没有找到伤疤。但是第林格的身上应该有几个旧枪伤。最后医生说死人的眼睛是棕色的。第林格的是蓝色的。

可能医生在检查第林格的身体时不彻底；也可能是警方击毙了另外一个人。我们不会确切地知道。我们所知道只是：在1934年7月22日以后约翰·第林格没有招惹过任何人。

---

companion *n.* 同伴；伴侣　　　　small-time *adj.* 三流的；无关轻重的
theory *n.* 推理；分析　　　　　　scar *n.* 伤痕

11

Assassin!

On April 4, 1968, Dr. Martin Luther King, Jr, went to Memphis, Tennessee. He checked into the Lorraine Motel. Early that evening, he *strolled* out onto the *balcony*. Some friends joined him there. Suddenly, from the shadows, someone fired a single *rifle* blast. A bullet smashed into Dr. King's neck. The bullet's

Grouped around Dr. Martin Luther King's body, his friends point to the source of the rifle shot that felled him. But the assassin had already fled.

刺客！

马丁·路德·金博士的朋友们聚集在他的身体旁，指着枪弹射来的方向。但是刺客已经逃跑了。

1968年4月4日，小马丁·路德·金博士来到了田纳西州的孟菲斯，住在了劳伦汽车旅馆。在那天傍晚，他在阳台上散步。他的一些朋友也在那里。突然从阴影处，有人开了一枪。一颗子弹打中了博士的颈部。子弹的力量如此地强大，以至于把他的领带打飞到了一边。在一个小时之内，

stroll *v.* 散步；闲逛
rifle *n.* 步枪

balcony *n.* 阳台

force was so great that it ripped the necktie right off him. Within an hour, Dr. King was dead. The death of this great African-American leader shocked the nation. Police quickly began a *massive* search for the assassin.

The police figured out that the *fatal* shot had come from a nearby rooming house. The *assassin* had been *sloppy*. He had left his rifle near the scene. The police were able to get a clear fingerprint off this weapon. They traced the print to a small-time crook named James Earl Ray.

James Earl Ray? Just the thought of Ray as an assassin baffled the police. What reason did he have to shoot Dr. King? He was not a known racist or King hater. In fact, James Earl Ray had never seemed like much of a threat to anyone. He had dropped out of high

---

金博士就去世了。这位伟大的美国黑人领袖的死使整个国家为之震惊。警方很快开始大规模搜捕刺客。

警方计算出这致命的一枪是从附近的一个卧室射出的。刺客有些大意。他把枪留在了现场附近。警方能够从枪上取得清晰的指纹。指纹使他们锁定在一个叫作詹姆斯·厄尔·雷的小流氓身上。

詹姆斯·厄尔·雷？他怎么能是刺客，这一点使警方很困惑。他杀金博士的原因是什么？他并不是一个为人所知的种族主义者或者金的仇人。实际上，詹姆斯·厄尔·雷看起来从来没有对任何人有威胁。他在中学10年级退学，曾经尝试过军旅生涯，但是没有成功。最后转向了犯罪的道路。

---

massive *adj.* 大规模的

assassin *n.* 刺客；暗杀者

fatal *adj.* 致命的

sloppy *adj.* 粗心的

school after 10th grade. He had tried army life, but with no success. *Eventually*, he had turned to a life of crime.

But Ray had not been very good at that, either. He once dropped his *wallet* during a robbery. That made it easy for police to prove he was the thief. Another time he was caught after falling out of a getaway car. His only "success" came in 1967. That year, he broke out of the Missouri State Prison. Even then, police were not exactly terrified. They put a *puny* $50 reward out for his capture.

And yet, his fingerprint was on the gun that killed Dr. King. So the police went looking for Ray. This time they set the reward at $100,000. But for the first time ever, they had trouble catching him. The man who had *botched* most of his other crimes now acted like a real, professional criminal.

　　但是雷做得也不是很好。他在一次抢劫中把自己的钱包掉了。这使警察很容易就证明他是窃贼。另一次他因从逃跑的车里面被甩下来而被捕。他唯一的一次成功是在1967年。那一年他从密苏里州立监狱逃跑。即使是这样，警方也丝毫没有害怕。他们因此提出悬赏区区50美元抓捕他。

　　但是，雷的指纹就出现在杀害金博士的枪支上。所有警方开始搜索雷。这次他们把奖金加到100,000美元。但是警方第一次在抓捕过程中遇到了困难。这个在大部分案子里面笨手笨脚的家伙这次倒像是一个真正的职业罪犯。

---

eventually *adv.* 最后；终于
puny *adj.* 微不足道的

wallet *n.* 钱包
botch *v.* 笨拙地做

First he fled to Toronto. There he *obtained* a Canadian passport. In those days that was easy to do. Ray simply paid $8 and swore that he was a Canadian citizen. The name he used was Ramon Sneyd.

Ray stayed in Canada for about a month. Then, on May 5, he used his *phony* passport to fly to England. He arrived in London on May 6. Soon after that, he flew to Portugal for five days. The reason for these trips has never been clear. Some people think Ray was just trying to *elude* police. Others think he was meeting someone who paid him to assassinate Dr. King. No one knows for sure.

Meanwhile, U.S. agents had picked up Ray's trail. They, too, knew how easy it was to get a Canadian passport. So they asked the police in Canada to sift through some 300,000 passport *applications*. At last, one officer found Ray's photo on a form for Ramon Sneyd.

首先他跑到了多伦多。在那里获得了加拿大的护照。那时，很容易得到。雷只支付了8美元并且发誓他是加拿大公民。他使用的名字是雷蒙·斯奈德。

雷大约在加拿大待了一个月。然后在5月5日使用一个假护照飞往英国，5月6日到达伦敦。很快他又逃到葡萄牙呆了5天。这些旅行的原因一直不清楚。有些人认为他就是在逃避警察。另一些人认为他在与雇用他刺杀金博士的人碰面。没有人知道确切的情况。

但是，美国的特工已经找到了他的踪迹。他们也知道很容易就能够得到加拿大的护照。所以他们请加拿大的警方详细审查300,000份护照申请材料。最后，一名警官发现雷的照片在雷蒙·斯奈德的申请表上。突然之

---

obtain *v.* 获得
elude *v.* 逃避；躲避

phony *adj.* 假的；伪造的
application *n.* 申请

Suddenly the *manhunt* heated up.

Back in England, Ray bounced from one cheap hotel to another. He must have known that the police were closing in. Using the name Sneyd, he called several newspapers. He asked how he could join some white army group in Africa. Ray must have thought he would be safe there. "Foreign legions" were famous for not asking about a person's history. One newspaper reporter suggested that Ray go to Belgium. Some white army groups were *recruiting* new soldiers there.

By now, however, the net had closed in on Ray. On June 8, "Sneyd" went to the airport. Just as he was about to board his plane to Belgium, the English police arrested him. They sent Ray back to the United States. He *pleaded* guilty and received a sentence of

间，这个搜索行动热了起来。

回到英格兰后，雷从一家廉价旅馆迁到另一家。他一定知道警察正在合围。他使用斯奈德的名字找了几家报纸，询问如何才能参加非洲的雇佣军。雷一定是以为他在那里能够安全。"海外兵团"以不调查参加者的历史而出名。一个报纸的记者建议雷到比利时去。那里有雇佣兵团在招兵。

现在这张网已经罩在了雷的身上。6月8日，"斯奈德"去了机场。就在他即将登上去往比利时的飞机时，英国警方逮捕了他。他们把斯奈德送回到美国。他承认有罪，被判处99年徒刑。在他被审判的第二天，雷又翻供。他想收回他承认的东西，声称他是被迫犯罪的。但是太晚了。已经

manhunt *n.* 搜捕；追捕　　　　　　recruit *v.* 招募；招聘
plead *v.* 申诉

99 years in prison. The day after he was sentenced, Ray changed his story. He tried to take back his plea, claiming that he had been forced to plead guilty. But it was too late. No one was listening.

For many people, the sentencing of James Earl Ray ended the story. But for others, questions remain. The most important one is this: Did Ray act alone? Agents for the U.S. government have always maintained that he did. But other people disagree. In 1978 a special *panel* studied the case. Panel members found a "*likelihood*" that other people were *involved*. James Earl Ray's own father said, "[James] couldn't have planned it alone. He wasn't smart enough for that."

If Ray did not act alone, then who helped him? Who told him what to do? Who planned—and paid for—his escape? No one knows. Some believe that a group of racists *masterminded* the killing.

没有人听了。

　　对许多人来说，对詹姆斯·厄尔·雷的审判结束了整个故事。但是对于另一些人来说，问题还是存在着。最重要的是: 雷是单独行动吗? 美国政府的特工们总是坚持说是的。但是另一些人不同意。1978年，一个特别委员会研究了这个案子。特别委员会发现了涉及其他人的"可能性"。詹姆斯·厄尔·雷的父亲说:"[詹姆斯]不可能自己独自计划，他没有那么高的智商。"

　　如果雷不是自己干的，那么谁帮助了他? 谁告诉他做什么? 谁策划了——并支付了他的逃亡? 没有人知道。一些人认为是一群种族主义者策划了这次刺杀。另一些人认为美国的领导人是幕后的黑手。按照这种理论，领导人不喜欢金博士，不喜欢他鼓动黑人群众的方式。

---

panel *n.* 小组委员会　　　　　　　　likelihood *n.* 可能性
involve *v.* 涉及；包含　　　　　　　mastermind *v.* 策划

Others think U.S. leaders were behind the plot. According to this theory, the leaders did not like Dr. King. They did not like the way he *stirred up* the African-American *community*.

If Ray did take *directions* from someone, why did he do it? What could have *persuaded* him to kill Dr. King? Many think his motive was simple. He wanted money. All the other crimes he had committed had been for money. According to one rumor, Ray was paid $50,000 for the murder. But like the other theories, this one has never been proven.

Many years have now passed since the assassination. James Earl Ray died in prison on April 23, 1998. The whole may never be known. But one fact remains. No one else has been charged in the murder of Dr. King. James Earl Ray is still the only one who ever served time for the assassination.

如果雷没有从任何人那里接受指使，他为什么这样做呢？是什么能够说服他去谋杀金博士？许多人认为他的目的很简单。他想要钱。所有其他的犯罪也都是为了钱。按照一个传言的说法，雷支付了50,000美元的罚金作为谋杀的处罚。但是同其他的理论一样，这个也从来没有被证明过。

从刺杀算起，许多年过去了。詹姆斯·厄尔·雷于1998年4月23日死于狱中。整个事件的真相可能永远无法知道。但是一个事实一直存在着。在金博士被谋杀后，没有任何其他的人被起诉。詹姆斯·厄尔·雷是唯一一个因这次刺杀而服刑的人。

---

stir up 激起；煽动   community *n.* 团体
direction *n.* 指示   persuade *v.* 说服；劝说

12

Machine Gun Kelly

The police called him Public Enemy Number One. His wife, Kathryn, *nicknamed* him "Machine Gun" Kelly. To be sure, George R. Kelly was a criminal. There is no doubt about that. And he certainly talked like a real *tough* guy. Kelly liked to *brag* that "no copper [police officer] will ever

George Kelly, an easygoing petty thief, got into real trouble when he kidnapped a rich oilman. Both "Machine Gun" Kelly and his wife, Kathryn, were given life sentences for the crime Kathryn masterminded.

"机枪" 凯利

　　乔治·凯利，是一个和气的小贼，当他绑架富有的石油商人时真正遇到了麻烦。"机枪"凯利和他的妻子凯塞林都因凯塞林策划的罪行而被判处终身监禁。

　　警方称他是"公众一号公敌"。他的妻子凯塞林叫他的外号"机枪"凯利。乔治·R·凯利是个确确实实的罪犯。这一点是没有疑问的。而且他的谈吐也如同一个真正的硬汉一样。凯利喜欢吹嘘说："没有警察能够

nickname *v.* 以绰号称呼
brag *v.* 吹牛；吹嘘

tough *adj.* 自信的；坚定的

take me alive." But was he all that bad? Was he the terror that the press made him out to be? Or was Kelly just an *easygoing* thief who happened to marry the wrong woman?

Kelly began his life of crime as a *bootlegger* during the 1920s.(A bootlegger is someone who sells illegal liquor.) But he wasn't very good at it.

The police usually caught him. They either kicked him out of town or gave him a few months in jail. As one person put it, Kelly was "a *good-natured slob*, a bootlegger who spilled more [liquor] than he delivered."

That changed in 1927, the year Kelly met Kathryn Shannon. Before their fateful meeting, Kelly didn't even like guns. And he never hurt anyone. But Kathryn was an ambitious and ruthless woman.

活着抓住我。"但是他真的那么坏吗？他有媒体说得那么可怕吗？还是凯利只是一名随和的小贼，恰巧娶了一个错误的女人？

在20世纪20年代，凯利以私酒贩子开始了他的犯罪生涯。但是他做得并不好。

警察总能抓住他。他们经常将凯利赶出城，或者把他在监狱中关上几个月。就如同一个人所说的那样，凯利是"一个脾气很好的笨蛋，一个撒的酒比运的酒还多的私酒贩子。"

这在1927年发生了变化，这一年，凯利遇到了凯塞林·珊农。在他们这次命运注定的相遇前，凯利甚至不喜欢使用枪，也是从来没有伤害过任何人。但是凯塞林是一个野心勃勃，毫无顾忌的人。不久她就看出来

---

easygoing *adj.* 随和的；随便的
good-natured 善良的；好脾气的

bootlegger *n.* 造私酒者
slob *n.* 笨蛋；懒虫

She soon saw that despite all the tough talk, George Kelly was really just a marshmallow. "You've got to be able to hurt people," she told him. "You've got to be tough or nobody will respect you."

Kathryn and Kelly were married, and she set out to *toughen* him up. She gave him a machine gun. She made him practice shooting *walnuts* off fence posts. In time, he became good enough to write his name on a wall with bullets. Kathryn also made sure that Kelly's *reputation* grew. She dreamed up phony stories about the big banks Kelly robbed. Kathryn even gave away empty bullet shells saying, "Have a *souvenir* of my husband, Machine Gun Kelly."

By 1931 Kelly had moved up the criminal ladder. The former bootlegger began to rob real banks. But he picked small country banks without much money. That was not good enough for Kathryn.

了，尽管乔治·凯利的谈吐很像个硬汉，但实际上，他就是个面瓜。"你要能打人，"她告诉凯利，"你要真正地自信起来，不然没有人会尊敬你。"

凯塞林和凯利结婚了，并开始训练他强硬起来。她给了凯利一把机关枪，并让他练习射击篱笆柱子上面放置的核桃。很快，他的枪法练得很好，可以在墙上用子弹打出自己的名字。凯塞林也让他的名气增长起来。她想象了一些关于凯利抢劫过大银行的故事。她甚至把一些空弹壳送人，说："给你一个我丈夫的纪念品，机枪凯利。"

1931年，凯利的犯罪生涯又进了一步。这一位前私酒贩子成了真正的银行劫匪。但是他选择了一些没太多钱的郊区银行。这对凯塞林来说

---

toughen *v.* 使变强壮
reputation *n.* 名声；声望

walnut *n.* 核桃；胡桃
souvenir *n.* 纪念品

She wanted to do something big. She had read stories about kidnappers getting huge *ransoms*. She began nagging Kelly to kidnap someone with lots of money. It was the only way to get rich, she insisted.

"Too *risky*," Kelly told her. But she kept pushing. Finally—as usual—Machine Gun Kelly gave in. He joined up with Albert Bates, another petty crook. They agreed to kidnap a rich Oklahoma City oilman named Charles Urschel.

On the night of July 22, 1933, Kelly and Bates broke into Urschel's home. They found the oilman and his wife playing cards with another couple. That *confused* Kelly. He was so *incompetent* that he hadn't bothered to find out what Urschel looked like. "Which one's Urschel?" he barked.

不够好。她想要干大生意。她读到了一些故事，说绑架者勒索了大笔的赎金，并开始与凯利唠叨，去绑架有钱的人，而且坚持这是唯一致富的途径。

"太冒险了，"凯利告诉她。但是她坚持鼓动他这么做。最后——和往常一样——机枪凯利屈服了。他和阿尔波特·巴茨，另一个小贼合伙，同意去绑架一名富有的俄克拉荷马城的石油商人查尔斯·厄其尔。

在1933年7月22日晚上，凯利和巴茨闯入了厄其尔的家，找到了石油商人和他的妻子，他们正在同另一对夫妇打牌。这使凯利很困惑。他是一个如此不称职的匪徒，以至于没有事先知道厄其尔的长相。"谁是厄其尔？"凯利吼叫着。

---

ransom *n.* 赎金
confuse *v.* 使糊涂；使困惑

risky *adj.* 冒险的
incompetent *adj.* 不胜任的；无能力的

Neither man answered. "All right," Kelly said at last, "we'll take both of you."

Kelly and Bates drove off with the two men. After a while, Kelly thought to look in their wallets. Only then did he *discover* who the real Urschel was. He and Bates *kicked* the other man out of the car, then continued on with the *blindfolded* Urschel.

They took the oilman to a *ranch* owned by Kathryn's parents in Paradise, Texas. From there, the Kellys demanded a ransom of $200,000. The Urschel family agreed to pay. But with Machine Gun Kelly in charge, collecting the money wasn't easy. Kelly missed one meeting because he couldn't get his car started. Finally, after eight days, he collected the ransom.

Kathryn now wanted to kill Urschel. For once in his life, Kelly

---

两个男人都没有回答。"好吧,"凯利最后说,"你们两个我都带走。"

凯利和巴茨带着两个人驾车离开。过了一会,凯利想起来看看他们的钱包。这时他才发现谁是真正的厄其尔。他和巴茨把另一个人踢下了车,然后带着蒙着黑布的厄其尔继续出发。

他们把石油商人带到了凯塞林父母在得克萨斯州帕拉迪斯的农场。在那里,凯利夫妇要求200,000美元的赎金。厄其尔一家同意支付。但是在机枪凯利控制的情况下,取钱也不容易。凯利因为汽车无法打火而错过了一次会面的机会。最后8天后,他取到了钱。

现在凯塞林想要杀死厄其尔。凯利一生中第一次站了出来与她对抗。

---

discover *v.* 发现
blindfolded *adj.* 被蒙住眼睛的

kick *v.* 踢
ranch *n.* 大农场

stood up to her. He *convinced* Bates and Kathryn to let Urschel go. Kelly pointed out that shooting him would "be bad for future business."

All this time, Charles Urschel had been alert and listening. The oilman had a *keen* memory. He noticed many *details* about his kidnapping. He hoped the police could later use these details to catch his captors. Urschel noted that the car ride had taken about 12 hours over *bumpy* roads. He also noticed that a plane passed overhead twice a day. He even figured out the times—9:15 A.M. and 5:45 P.M..

After his release, Urschel gave these facts to agents from the Federal Bureau of Investigation (FBI). They knew what the 12-hour ride over bumpy roads meant. It meant the ranch was within 300 miles of Oklahoma City. The agents also studied hundreds of flight

---

他说服巴茨和凯塞林让厄其尔走，并指出毙了他"对以后的生意不利"。

所有这一切，查尔斯·厄其尔都在倾听。这位石油商人的思维很敏锐。并注意到许多他们绑架的细节，他希望日后警方能够通过这些细节抓住这些绑匪。厄其尔注意到，汽车大约在颠簸的路面上行驶了12小时，还注意到每天飞机经过头顶两次。他甚至计算出了时间——上午9:15和下午5:45。

在他获释后，厄其尔把这些要点提供给联邦调查局的探员。他们知道12个小时的颠簸路面意味着什么。它意味着离俄克拉荷马城300英里以内的一个农场。特工们还研究了成百上千的飞机航线。他们发现每天上午

---

convince *v.* 说服
detail *n.* 细节

keen *adj.* 敏锐的
bumpy *adj.* 颠簸的；崎岖不平的

plans. They found the spot where daily flights crossed at 9:15 A.M. and 5:45 P.M. That spot was Paradise.

The FBI was now hot on the trail of Machine Gun Kelly. Agents *labeled* him Public Enemy Number One. Kelly and his wife ran, but they couldn't hide. *Investigators* tracked them down at a cheap hotel in Memphis, Tennessee. Three police officers burst into Kelly's room. One shoved a shotgun into Kelly's stomach. Poor old Machine Gun gave up without a fight. "I've been waiting for you all night," he said softly.

At their trial, Kathryn turned against her husband. She tried to put all the blame on him. No one listened. Machine Gun, Kathryn, and Bates all got life sentences. It was a *pitiful* end for this *so-called* tough guy. Prison life at Leavenworth and Alcatraz was hard on George

---

9:15和下午5:45都有飞机经过的地点，就是帕拉迪斯。

现在联邦调查局开始密切跟踪机枪凯利。特工把他标记为"公众一号公敌"。凯利和他的妻子跑了，但是他们无处可藏。侦探们追踪到了田纳西州孟菲斯的一家廉价旅馆。三名警察冲进了凯利的房间。其中一个用步枪顶住凯利的肚子。可怜的老机枪凯利没有抵抗就投降了。"整个晚上我都在等待着你们，"他有气无力地说。

在审判中，凯塞林把一切都推在凯利身上，想让他承担所有罪责。没有人听她的谎言。机枪凯利、凯塞林和巴茨都被判处无期徒刑。对于这个所谓的硬汉来说，这个命运是悲惨的。"机枪"乔治·凯利在利文沃斯和

---

label *v.* 给······加标签　　　　　　　　investigator *n.* 侦探；探员
pitiful *adj.* 可怜的　　　　　　　　　　so-called *adj.* 所谓的

Machine Gun Kelly. His *fellow inmates* often laughed at him. They even gave him a new nickname— "Pop Gun" Kelly.

Just before he died in 1954, Kelly wrote a letter to his *former* victim, Charles Urschel. "These five words seem written in fire on the walls of my *cell*," Kelly wrote. "Nothing can be worth this!" He might have said the same thing about his marriage to Kathryn.

阿尔塔克拉斯的狱中生活很难。同室的狱友笑话他，甚至给他起了一个新的外号——"玩具枪"凯利。

就在凯利1954年去世前，他给他的前受害者查尔斯·厄其尔写了一封信。"这五个词好像是用我囚室墙壁上的火写成的，"凯利写道，"这个代价太重了！"可能他对于同凯塞林的婚姻也是这么说的。

---

fellow *adj.* 同伴的；同道的
former *adj.* 先前的；旧时的

inmate *n.* （监狱、精神病院等）被收容者
cell *n.* 小牢房

13

The Man with Many Faces

His parents named him Stephen Jacob Weinberg, but he *rarely* used that name. Weinberg, who was born in Brooklyn in 1890, loved to make up new names for himself. He loved to *pretend* he was someone with an important job. Often he used the name Stanley Clifford Weyman or something

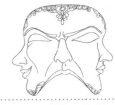

This man could be a Serbian army officer, a Romanian diplomat, a U.S. Army pilot, a doctor, or a prison reform expert. Talented impostor Stephen Jacob Weinberg could convince people that he could be and do almost anything.

多面人

　　这个人可能是塞尔维亚军官，也可能是罗马尼亚外交官、美国陆军飞行员、医生、监狱改革专家。这位富有天分的冒名顶替者斯蒂芬·雅各布·温博格能够说服人们相信他能够做任何事情。

　　他的父母给他起名斯蒂芬·雅各布·温博格，但是他很少用这个名字。这位1890年出生于布卢克林的温博格喜欢给自己起一些新名字。他喜欢假装是有重要职位的人，而且经常使用的名字是斯坦利·克立弗得·

rarely　*adv.* 很少

pretend　*v.* 假装

close to it. For nearly forty years, Weinberg played all sorts of make-believe roles. This daring *impostor* fooled most people. But sooner or later, someone always found out who he really was. Sometimes the police let him off with a warning. Other times he went to jail.

Weinberg was a bright young man. With some hard work, he might have become a doctor or a pilot or a *diplomat* or a *navy* officer. But Weinberg had two problems. First, he lacked the *patience* to go to college and study for any of these professions. Second, he wanted to hold all these jobs. He decided there was only one thing to do. He would pretend to be whatever he wanted. That way he could be a doctor one day and something else the next.

Being a good impostor isn't easy. Weinberg quickly learned how hard it could be. In 1912 he posed as "Clifford Weinberg, the

---

维曼或者相近的什么。在近40年间，温博格一直在做这种假冒的角色。这个大胆的冒名顶替者愚弄了大多数的人。但是迟早人们会知道他的真实身份。有时警方给他一个警告就把他放了，但还有时，他就要入狱。

温博格是一个聪明的年轻人。如果他努力工作，就可能成为医生，或者飞行员、外交官，或海军军官。但是温博格有两个毛病。首先，他缺乏上大学学习其中任何一个专业的耐心。第二，他想拥有所有这些工作。他决定，只有一件事可以做。他将假装是他想成为的人。这样，一天他可以是医生，第二天是另一个什么。

做一名好的假冒者并不容易。温博格很快就知道那有多么难。1912年，他假装是"克立弗得·温博格，美国驻摩洛哥领事"。早些时候，他

---

impostor *n.* 冒充者
navy *n.* 海军

diplomat *n.* 外交官
patience *n.* 耐性；耐心

American Consul to Morocco." Earlier, Weinberg had stolen a camera from a photographer's shop. One day the shop owner showed up at a photo *session* for "*consul*" Weinberg. The owner recognized the "consul" as a thief, and Weinberg ended up in jail.

After he got out, Weinberg tried to get honest work. But every job he got seemed dull next to the jobs he dreamed up in his head. So Weinberg went back to his *fantasies*. He became "Lieutenant Royale St. Cyr," a U.S. Army pilot. He also took on the role of a U.S. Navy officer. For a while, he posed as an army officer from Serbia. He also became "Ethan Allen Weinberg," a diplomat from Romania. Some people said Weinberg looked good in a *military uniform*. He must have—he certainly wore enough of them! He also wore plenty of prison uniforms. Between 1913 and 1918, he was in and out of jail at

---

曾经从一家照相馆偷过一个相机。一天店主出现在照相会议中，见到"领事"温博格，并认出领事是个小偷，温博格因此入狱。

出狱后，他试着找了一份诚实的工作。但是他得到的每一份工作看起来都很枯燥，工作的同时，他的头脑中又形成了一个新的想法。这样温博格又回到了他的梦幻中。他成为"罗耶尔·圣·塞尔"，一名美军的飞行员，同时扮演着美国海军军官的角色。有一段时间他假装是从塞尔维亚来的军官。一些人说温博格穿军装的样子很好看。他一定——他必然穿够了军装！他同样也穿够了囚服。在1913年至1918年间，他至少入狱4次。

---

session *n.* 正式会议

fantasy *n.* 幻想；梦想

consul *n.* 领事

military uniform 军装

least four times.

By 1920 Weinberg was ready for another *challenge*. A New York company needed a doctor to go to Peru. The doctor would check out health *conditions* at a work site there. A "Dr. Clifford Wyman"applied for the job. Like all the other applicants, he was *interviewed* by a real doctor. "Dr. Wyman" completely fooled the interviewer. He made such a good *impression* that he got the job.

Soon "Dr. Wyman" set sail for Peru. There he rented a fancy house, bought a nice car, and gave huge parties. He had all his bills sent to the company back in New York. The local workers liked "Dr. Wyman" very much. And why not? He simply approved everything they did. But at last, company officials found out who "Dr. Wyman" really was. They fired him but didn't press charges. Perhaps they

---

1920年，温博格做好准备接受另一个挑战。一个纽约的公司需要一名派往秘鲁的医生。医生要在那里的办公点检查健康情况。"克立弗得·维曼医生"申请了这份工作。和其他申请者一起，一名真的医生给他们进行面试。"维曼医生"完全愚弄了面试者。他留下了很好的印象，获得了这份工作。

很快，"维曼医生"出发去了秘鲁。他在那里租了一栋豪华住宅，买了一辆好车，开办大型的宴会。他把所有的账单都送回纽约的公司。当地的工人十分喜欢"维曼医生"。为什么不呢？他只是对他们所有的事情都表示同意。但是最后公司的管理人员发现了"维曼医生"的真实身份，并

---

challenge *n.* 挑战
interview *v.* 对某人进行面试

condition *n.* 条件；状况；环境
impression *n.* 印象

were too embarrassed about hiring him in the first place!

In 1921 Princess Fatima of Afghanistan arrived in New York. She hoped to meet U.S. President Warren Harding. And she did. The meeting was set up by someone dressed as a *naval* officer. He said his name was "Sterling Clifford Wyman." No one questioned "Wyman." He seemed to know exactly what he was doing. He even got the *princess* to pay for all his *expenses*. (He told her it was an American custom.) She finally smartened up when "Wyman" offered to help her sell her *priceless* forty-two-carat diamond. Later, the police caught on as well. Weinberg was arrested and charged with impersonating a navy officer. He was sent to prison for two years.

Still, Weinberg refused to quit role-playing. He loved the thrill

---

开除了他，但是没有提起诉讼。可能是他们对一开始雇用他感到很尴尬！

1921年，阿富汗的法提马公主到达纽约。她希望能够与美国总统沃伦·哈丁会面。她终于见到了。这次会面是由一个穿着美国海军军官服装的人操持的。他说他叫"斯特林·克立弗得·维曼"。没有人对"维曼"提出疑问。看起来他非常了解他的工作，甚至让公主支付了他的所有费用。（他告诉她说这是美国的习俗。）当"维曼"表示帮助出售她的42克拉的无价钻石时，公主终于聪明起来了。后来警方也参与了进来。温博格被捕，他被以假冒海军军官的罪名起诉。这次他入狱两年。

但是，温博格拒绝退出这个假扮角色的行业。他喜欢其中的刺激。一

---

naval *adj.* 海军的　　　　　　　　　princess *n.* 公主
expense *n.* 消费；花费　　　　　　　priceless *adj.* 无价的；极贵重的

of it. A little jail time seemed a small price to pay for such *grand adventures*. Once, Weinberg even tried to pass himself off as a "prison reform expert." There was just one problem. His old prison *warden* recognized him! Another time, Weinberg started up his own law office. But since he had no license to practice law, that led to another term behind bars.

During World War II, Weinberg began calling himself a "Selective Service consultant." That sounded pretty good. But what Weinberg was doing was illegal. He was teaching young men how to *avoid* serving in the army. He taught them, for example, how to fake deafness. Again, he was caught and sent to prison.

Weinberg got out of jail in 1948. He decided to become a reporter. As "Stanley Clifford Weyman," he got a job with the Erwin

---

点点的入狱时间看起来是这个伟大冒险的一点点代价。一次，温博格甚至把自己装扮成"监狱改革专家"。只是有一个问题，他的老看守认识他！还有一次温博格自己开设了律师事务所。但是因为他没有从事法律职业的执照，便又入狱了。

在二战期间，温博格开始自称"选择性服役顾问"。这个工作听起来不错。但是所做的却是违法的事。他教授年轻人如何躲避服兵役。比如他教他们如何假装耳聋。这次他又被捕入狱。

1948年，温博格出狱。他决定成为一名记者。以"斯坦利·克立弗得·维曼"的名字，他获得了一份俄尔文新闻社的工作。他的工作是报道

---

grand *adj.* 极好的；美妙的　　　　adventure *n.* 冒险
warden *n.* 看守人　　　　　　　　avoid *v.* 避免

News Service. His task was to cover the United Nations. Mr. Erwin later said, "Weyman had good news sense—and he seemed to know everybody."

"Weyman" was so good, in fact, that he got his own radio show on WFDR. Every day he gave a five-minute comment on the news. Once a week he had special guests join him on the show. They included top diplomats from all over the world. Some diplomats from Thailand were *especially* impressed with him. ("Weyman" had convinced them that he had worked as a *spy* on their *behalf* during World War II.) In 1951 the Thais offered "Weyman" a job as their own press officer. For Weinberg this was a dream come true. He would now be a real diplomat.

But, as usual, Weinberg was caught. He started *wondering* how

---

联合国。俄尔文先生后来说，"维曼有很好的新闻感觉——而且他好像认识每个人。"

"维曼"工作得太好了，实际上，他甚至出现在WFDR的无线电广播中。每天他都对新闻发表5分钟的评论。每周会有一名特殊的客人加入到节目中来。他们是全世界的顶级外交官。尤其是一些来自于泰国的外交官对他留有很深的印象。（"维曼"说服他们，在二战期间，他曾经是他们的间谍。）1951年，泰国人为"维曼"提供了一份泰国新闻官的工作。对于温博格来说，他的梦想实现了。现在他可以是一名真正的外交官了。

但是，和往常一样，温博格还是被抓住了。他开始考虑这个工作对他

---

especially *adv.* 特别；尤其
behalf *n.* 代表某人

spy *n.* 间谍
wonder *v.* 想知道

the job would affect him as an American citizen. So he wrote a letter to the State *Department* asking about it. Officials there checked into Weinberg's *background*. It isn't hard to guess the rest of the story. The embarrassed Thais *withdrew* the job offer. And Weinberg lost his job with the Erwin News Service.

By 1960 Weinberg was an old man. He took a job working as a night *clerk* in a New York hotel. But he still had dreams of glory. One night two gunmen came in to rob the cash box. Weinberg had no weapon, but he tried to fight off the robbers anyway. The gunmen shot him, then fled without the money. As Weinberg lay dying, perhaps he took some comfort in knowing his last role in life was that of a hero.

的美国公民身份是否有影响。所以他给国务院写信询问这件事。官员们查到了温博格的背景。剩下的故事就容易猜到了。很尴尬的泰国人撤回了他们提供的工作职位。而且温博格也失去了在俄尔文新闻社的工作。

1960年，温博格已经是个老人了。他在一家纽约旅馆做一名夜间值班。但是他还是有着光荣的梦想。一天晚上，两名持枪匪徒闯入抢劫钱箱。温博格没有武器，但是他还是与匪徒尽力搏斗。持枪匪徒开枪击毙了他，没有抢到钱就逃跑了。当温博格倒地奄奄一息的时候，如果他知道他这一生的最后一个角色是英雄的话，他会感到很欣慰的。

---

department *n.* 部门
withdraw *v.* 收回

background *n.* 背景
clerk *n.* 店员

Was Lizzie Borden an Axe Murderer?

Lizzie Borden took an *axe* and gave her mother forty whacks. When she saw what she had done, she gave her father forty-one.

This *rhyme* has been around for more than a hundred years. It *describes* Lizzie Borden as a cold-blooded killer. But is the rhyme *accurate*? Did Lizzie butcher

Neighbors said that Lizzie Borden was kind and gentle. Yet when her father and stepmother were found murdered in their home, suspicion focused on Lizzie. She was the only one home at the time. Didn't she hear or see anything?

斧头杀手

邻居们都说里奇·伯顿友好而且温柔。但是当她的父亲和继母双双在家里被杀时，怀疑被集中到里奇的身上。当时她是唯一一个在家的人。她没有听到或看到什么吗？

里奇·伯顿拿起了一把斧子砍了她母亲40下，当她看到她的所作所为时，她又砍了她父亲41下。

这句诗已经流传了100多年。她描写了里奇·伯顿，作为一个冷血杀手的样子。但是这首诗写得准确吗？里奇是在1892年一个炎热8月的早晨杀害了她的父母双亲吗？还是有别人干的这个谋杀？

---

axe *n.* 斧（子）
describe *v.* 描述

rhyme *n.* 韵文；诗
accurate *adj.* 精确的

her parents one hot August morning in 1892? Or did someone else commit the *brutal* murders?

The crimes took place in Fall River, Massachusetts. That's where thirty-two-year-old Lizzie Borden lived with her father, *stepmother*, and older sister, Emma. The morning of August 4, 1892, began quietly enough in the Borden house. Mr. Borden left for work around 9 A.M. Mrs. Borden started to do her housework. The maid, Bridget Sullivan, went outside to wash windows. Emma was away. She was visiting friends in a nearby town. And Lizzie? Well, Lizzie said she spent much of the morning out in the barn. She was getting things ready for a fishing trip she planned to take. The rest of the time, she said, she was in her room, lying down.

Sometime between 9 and 9:30 A.M., Mrs. Borden was making

这次犯罪发生在马萨诸塞的法尔河，32岁的里奇·伯顿和她的父亲、继母和姐姐一起生活在这里。1892年的8月4日，伯顿一家静静地开始了新的一天。早晨9点，伯顿先生出门上班。伯顿夫人开始做一天的家务活。女仆布里吉特·苏立文到外面去清洗窗户。爱玛出去了。她到附近的城镇去拜访朋友。里奇呢？里奇说她大部分的上午时间是在谷仓里，正在准备她打算参加的钓鱼旅行。其他的时间，她在自己的房间里面，倒在床上。

大约在上午9:00至9:30分之间，伯顿夫人在二楼的卧室里铺床。有人

---

brutal *adj.* 残忍的　　　　　　　　　　stepmother *n.* 继母

a bed in a second-floor bedroom. Someone crept into the room behind her. Without warning, the killer brought an axe down on Mrs. Borden's head. Nineteen times she was struck with the axe. Blood *splattered* all over the walls. By the time the killer was finished, Mrs. Borden lay dead. Her body was not found right away, however. When Mr. Borden came home around 10:30 A.M., he had no idea that anything was wrong.

Mr. Borden headed straight for the couch in the sitting room. He had not been feeling well, and the *sweltering* heat of the morning had *drained* his energy. He wanted to rest awhile. The maid was also feeling sick that day. A *nap* sounded like a good idea to her, too. Accordingly, Bridget Sullivan went up to her attic room and quickly fell asleep.

在她身后溜进了房间。在毫无警示的情况下，杀手用斧子击中了伯顿太太的头部。她身中19斧。鲜血溅到了墙上。当杀手停止的时候，伯顿夫人已经倒地身亡。她的尸体在那里，没有人发现。当伯顿先生10:30回来时，全然不知发生了什么。

伯顿先生直接走到了起居室，坐在沙发上。他当时的感觉并不好，上午的闷热使他筋疲力尽。他想要休息一会。女仆那一天也感觉不好，想休息一会。当时布里吉特·苏立文回到了她在顶楼的房间，马上就睡着了。

---

splatter *v.* 溅泼
drain *v.* 耗尽

sweltering *adj.* 闷热的
nap *n.* 小睡

Once again the killer sprang into *action*. Before Mr. Borden knew what was happening, an axe *struck* him in the face. The killer delivered ten blows, leaving Mr. Borden—like his wife—dead in the house.

At 11:15 A.M. Lizzie Borden screamed to Bridget Sullivan. "Come down quick! Someone's killed Father!" With those words, Lizzie *announced* the *horrible* news. Soon neighbors, police officers, and reporters were swarming around the Borden home. One of the neighbors discovered Mrs. Borden's body in the upstairs bedroom. By evening, Lizzie's sister Emma had heard the news. She hurried home to be with Lizzie.

Meanwhile, questions swirled through the community. Who could have done such terrible deeds? And why? Suspicion centered on

---

杀手再次行动。伯顿先生还没有意识到发生了什么事情的时候，斧子已经击中了他的脸。杀手砍了十下，伯顿先生也如同他的妻子一样倒在房间里面，死了。

在上午11:15，里奇·伯顿尖声叫着布里吉特·苏立文。"快下来！有人杀死了爸爸！"里奇用这句话宣布了可怕的消息。很快邻居、警察、记者团团围住了伯顿的家。一个邻居发现伯顿夫人的尸体在楼上的房间里。晚上，里奇的姐姐爱玛也听到了这个消息。她马上回到了家里，和里奇待在了一起。

当时，整个邻里都在回旋着一个问题。是谁干的这个可怕的事情？而

---

action *n.* 行动
announce *v.* 宣布

strike *v.* 打；击
horrible *adj.* 可怕的

Lizzie. Her story didn't make sense. She said she had been out in the barn, but there were no *footprints* on the *dusty* barn floor. It looked to police as though no one had set foot in there for days or even weeks. In addition, the maid reported an interesting detail. When Mr. Borden came home that morning, Lizzie had stood at the top of the stairs, laughing in an *odd* way. And several hours after the murders, Lizzie was seen burning a piece of wood that looked like an axe handle.

Besides, many people *whispered*, no one else could have done it. The doors to the house were locked, so no intruder could have gotten in. Everyone knew that Lizzie hated her stepmother. And with Mr. and Mrs. Borden both dead, Lizzie and her sister would inherit half a million dollars.

且为什么呢？疑点集中在里奇身上。她的故事毫无意义。她说她曾经在谷仓里，但是在充满灰尘的谷仓地面上没有脚印。在警方看来已经有好几天或者几个星期没有人到过那里了。而且女仆报告了一个有趣的细节。当伯顿先生那天上午回来时，里奇站在楼梯的顶部，非常奇怪地笑着。而且在谋杀发生的几个小时后，看到里奇在烧一块木头，看起来好像是斧头柄。

　　而且，许多人窃窃私语，没有别人能干这件事。房子的门是锁着的，没有人能够随便闯入。每个人都知道里奇恨她的继母。如果伯顿夫妇双双去世，里奇和她的姐姐可以继承50万美元的财产。

---

footprint *n.* 足迹；脚印　　　　　　dusty *adj.* 落满灰尘的
odd *adj.* 奇怪的　　　　　　　　　whisper *v.* 窃窃私语；私下传说

Yet some questions could not be answered. There was blood all over the crime *scenes*. So how could it be that no blood was found on Lizzie or her clothing? If Lizzie were the killer, where had she *hidden* the murder weapon? And how could she have stayed so calm during the hour between the two killings?

Some people decided that Lizzie's sister, Emma, was the murderer. She, too, hated her stepmother. In fact, Emma hated Mrs. Borden even more than Lizzie did. Lizzie was just a baby when her real mother died. But Emma was eleven years old. She was old enough to remember her mother—and to hate the woman who tried to *replace* her. Like Lizzie, Emma knew she would get a lot of money when her parents died. And although Emma had been staying with friends on the day of the murders, she could easily have *sneaked*

　　但是有一些问题无法得到回答。在犯罪的现场遍布鲜血，但是怎么在里奇的身上、衣服上面一点血迹也找不到？如果里奇是谋杀的凶手，她把谋杀的武器藏到哪里去了呢？而且在两次谋杀之间的几个小时中她怎么能那么平静呢？

　　还有一些人认定是里奇的姐姐爱玛干的。她也恨她的继母。实际上，爱玛比里奇还要恨继母。当她们真正的母亲去世时，里奇还是一个婴儿，可爱玛已经11岁大了。她的年龄足以记住她的妈妈了——而且憎恨那个取代她妈妈位置的女人。与里奇一样，爱玛也知道，如果她的父母死了，她们可以继承许多钱。而且尽管在谋杀当天，爱玛与她的朋友们待在一起，

---

scene *n.* 现场
replace *v.* 取代；替代

hide *v.* 隐藏
sneak *v.* 溜进；潜行

back into town. She had a key to the house. She would have had no trouble unlocking the door.

Other people believed both sisters were *innocent*. After all, neither one had ever been violent before. They had always been kind and gentle. The Borden house had been broken into a few months earlier. Perhaps the thief had returned, this time with murder in mind. Or what about the enemies Mr. Borden had made in his business dealings? The killer could have been someone seeking *revenge*. A stranger could have slipped into the house while Lizzie was in the barn. During that time, the door was unlocked.

The police were in a difficult spot. The *entire* nation was watching the events in Fall River. Most police officers believed Lizzie was the killer. But they had no *witness*, no murder weapon, and no real evidence. It would be hard to make a case. Still, there was

---

但是她可以很容易地潜回来。她有房子的钥匙，开门是没有问题的。

　　还有一些人认为，姊妹两个都是无辜的。毕竟她们以前都没有粗暴过，总是友好而且温柔。几个月前，伯顿的住房被窃贼光顾过，可能是窃贼又回来了，这次是带着谋杀的念头回来的。或者是伯顿先生生意中的敌人？杀手可能是来复仇的。可能是在里奇待在谷仓中时，一个陌生人潜入了房子。那段时间，门没有锁。

　　警方处于一个困难的境地。全国都在注视着法尔河发生的事件。大部分的警官认为里奇是杀人凶手。但是他们没有目击者，没有谋杀凶器，没有真实的证据。很难立案。而且又有强大的压力要求他们进行逮捕。在谋

---

innocent *adj.* 无辜的
entire *adj.* 全部的；整个的

revenge *n.* 复仇；报复
witness *n.* 证人；目击者

tremendous pressure on them to make an arrest. One week after the killings, they did. They arrested Lizzie Borden and charged her with two counts of murder.

The trial took place in June of 1893. It lasted thirteen days. Both sides did their best. But in the end, the jury simply could not believe that the calm, quiet Lizzie Borden had committed such *awful* acts. They spent one hour *discussing* the case. Then they found Lizzie not guilty.

In many ways, though, the jury's verdict did not matter. Lizzie's life was changed forever. Most people believed she was guilty. To this day, Lizzie Borden is not remembered for her love of animals. She is not remembered for the money she gave to the poor. She is remembered only as the woman who gave her mother "forty whacks" and then went on to give her father "forty-one".

杀事件后的一个星期，他们逮捕了里奇·伯顿并以两项谋杀罪起诉了她。

审判于1893年6月进行，延续了13天。双方都尽了最大的努力。但是最后，陪审团就是不相信平静、沉默的里奇·伯顿能够做出这样可怕的事情来。他们花费了一个小时来讨论这个案件。然后他们认为里奇无罪。

但是，陪审团的裁定在许多方面是没有用处的。里奇的生活从此永远地改变了。大部分的人认为她是有罪的。直到今天，里奇·伯顿不是因为她爱小动物而为人们记住，也不是因为她给过穷人钱。她为人们所知，仅仅因为她砍了她母亲"40斧"，然后又砍了她父亲"41斧"。

---

tremendous *adj.* 极大的
awful *adj.* 可怕的

pressure *n.* 压力
discuss *v.* 讨论

15

A Nazi War Criminal

On the list of the world's worst criminals, Adolf Eichmann has to rank near the top. He was not just an *ordinary* criminal. He was a war criminal. Eichmann sent six million people to their deaths during World War II. Most frightening of all is that in his own *warped* mind, Eichmann

Protected by a wall of bulletproof glass, former Nazi Adolf Eichmann listens to testimony of concentration camp survivors during his trial for the murder of 6 million people.

纳粹战犯

前纳粹党徒阿道夫·埃克曼在集中营杀害了六百万人。在法庭上，他在防弹玻璃的保护下接受集中营幸存者的控诉。

在世界上最坏的罪犯列表中，阿道夫·埃克曼处于前排位置。他不是一个普通的罪犯。他是一名战犯。埃克曼在二战期间杀害了六百万人。最可怕的是他在自己扭曲的思维中，认为他在做着正确的事。

ordinary *adj.* 普通的   warped *adj.* 弯曲的；古怪的

thought he was doing the right thing.

Eichmann's road to *evil* began in 1932. That was when he joined the Nazi party. The Nazis were led by Adolf Hitler, a vile madman who wanted to take over Europe. Along the way, Hitler hoped to wipe out all the *Jews* living there. Eichmann worked his way up in Germany's Nazi party. He rose to a position of great power. He became a *specialist* in what Hitler called the "Jewish problem." In other words, Eichmann was in charge of killing Jews.

Eichmann carried out his *hateful* work from 1938 to 1945. These were the years just before and during World War II. During this time, Germany controlled most of Europe. So millions of Jews from France to Poland came under Nazi rule. Eichmann began rounding them up and sending them to their deaths. "When I am finished with my

埃克曼的罪恶之路开始于1932年。当时他加入了纳粹党。纳粹党在阿道夫·希特勒的领导之下，使他成为一个妄图占领整个欧洲的疯子。希特勒希望顺便消灭所有在那里居住的犹太人。埃克曼在德国纳粹党中的地位节节高升，并被提拔到一个掌管巨大权力的位置。他成为一个希特勒所称的"犹太问题"专家。换句话说，他掌管着屠杀犹太人的大权。

埃克曼在1938年至1945年执行着这个令人厌恶的工作。这包括二战前和二战期间。当时，德国控制着大部分欧洲。所以从法兰西到波兰数以百万计的犹太人处于纳粹的统治之下。埃克曼把他们包围起来，集中杀掉。"我的工作如果胜利结束，"他大肆吹嘘道，"欧洲就不再存在犹太人。"

evil *n.* 罪恶；邪恶
specialist *n.* 专家

Jew *n.* 犹太人
hateful *adj.* 可憎的；讨厌的

work," he once bragged, "there will be no more Jews in Europe."

Eichmann shipped his victims to *concentration camps*. There, anyone who was not able to work was immediately killed. The old, the young, and the sick were sent directly to *gas chambers*. The rest were forced to work like slaves. A sign over the gate of one camp read, "Work Brings Freedom". That was a cruel *hoax*. The Nazis' real goal was to work Jews until they couldn't work anymore. Then those Jews, too, were killed. By 1945 Adolf Eichmann and his *henchmen* had murdered six million Jews.

Hitler and the Nazis were finally defeated in 1945. As the war ended, Adolf Hitler killed himself. Other Nazi leaders were caught and put on trial for their war crimes. Most were hanged. But a few top Nazi leaders got away. One of them was Eichmann. In a strange

---

埃克曼把他的受害者运输到集中营。在那里凡是不能工作的人马上处决。年老的、年幼的、生病的人马上被送进了毒气室。剩下的做着奴隶一般的工作。一个集中营的大门上写着："工作带来自由"。这是一个残酷的愚弄。纳粹党真实的目的是利用犹太人，直到他们不能再工作为止。然后这些犹太人同上处理，杀掉。到1945年为止，阿道夫·埃克曼和他忠诚的跟随者们已经谋杀了六百万犹太人。

希特勒及其纳粹党徒在1945年被击败。随着战争的结束，阿道夫·希特勒自杀身亡。其他纳粹领导人被捕，被审判。大部分被执行绞刑。但是有一小部分纳粹领导人逃跑了。埃克曼就是他们其中之一。一次十分偶

---

concentration camp 集中营   gas chamber 毒气室
hoax *n.* 骗局   henchman *n.* 追随者；帮凶

twist of fate, Eichmann was captured at first. But no one knew who he was. He had disguised himself in a uniform stolen from a dead German soldier. He was put in a *prisoner-of-war* camp along with other low-ranking German soldiers. Before anyone figured out his true *identity*, he escaped.

The police from many countries searched for Eichmann. He was at the top of the Most Wanted War Criminal list. Still, no one could find him. He had vanished. After a few years, most people stopped looking. But Jewish *investigators* never gave up. From 1945 on, they continued their search. In 1948 Jews created their own nation, called *Israel*. The Israeli police sent secret agents around the world looking for Eichmann. For many years, they had no luck. Then in 1960 they got a break. Someone looking just like Eichmann was spotted in

---

然的机遇，埃克曼曾经被抓住。但是没有人知道他是谁。他从一名死去的德国士兵身上偷了一件军装，伪装得很像。他和其他德国低等级士兵一起被关进了战俘营。在人们能够找出他的真实身份之前，他逃跑了。

许多国家的警察在搜索埃克曼。他被列于"最重要的战犯"的首位。但是没有人能够找到他。他消失了。一些年后，大部分人已经停止寻找。但是犹太调查员们从来就没有放弃。从1945年开始，他们继续着他们的搜索。1948年，犹太人建立了他们自己的国家，叫作以色列。以色列警方派秘密侦探到世界各地去搜索埃克曼。多年以来，他们运气不好。然而在1960年，他们得到转机。一个看起来酷似埃克曼的人在南美被发现。

---

prisoner-of-war 战俘
investigator *n.* 调查者

identity *n.* 身份
Israel *n.* 以色列

South America.

Israel sent secret agents to Buenos Aires, the capital of Argentina. They tracked down the man in question. It was Eichmann! He was living under the name Ricardo Clement and working in a local auto plant. The agents were *eager* to grab him. They wanted to take him to Israel to stand *trial* for his war crimes. But they had to be careful. If Eichmann realized they were on his trail, he might disappear again. Then they would have to start the search all over.

There was one other problem. Israel had no *treaty* with Argentina about turning over war criminals. So Argentine police could not be counted on to help the Israeli agents. In fact, the police might try to protect Eichmann. The Israelis decided they would have to kidnap Eichmann. Then somehow they would *smuggle* him out of the country.

以色列派秘密侦探到了布宜诺斯艾利斯阿根廷的首都。他们跟踪着那个有问题的人。他就是埃克曼！他使用一个新的名字："理查多·克莱曼"，在当地的一家汽车工厂工作。侦探们很想抓住他，并想要把他送回以色列去审判他的战争罪行。但是他们要小心。如果埃克曼发觉他们在跟踪，就会再次消失。那么他们就要重新开始了。

还有一个问题。以色列和阿根廷之间没有交换战犯的协定。所以不能指望阿根廷的警察来帮助以色列的侦探。实际上，当地警方可能尽量保护埃克曼。以色列人决定绑架埃克曼。然后再使用什么方法把他偷运出国。

---

eager *adj.* 渴望的

treaty *n.* 条约

trial *n.* 审讯；审判

smuggle *v.* 走私；偷运

On May 11, 1960, the agents set their trap. They followed Eichmann as he left work. As he walked down the street, a car pulled up beside him and suddenly stopped. Four men jumped out. Eichmann saw them and started to scream. But one of the agents clubbed him over the head. The agents tossed the *unconscious* Eichmann into the back seat of the car, and the car sped away. The agents then sent a secret message back to Israel: "The beast is in chains."

The agents took Eichmann to a *hideout* a few miles from Buenos Aires. Eichmann thought they were going to murder him on the spot. "Don't kill me!" he begged. "Please don't kill me!" But the agents had no *intention* of killing Eichmann. Instead, on May 19, they slipped him onto a *chartered* plane and took off for Israel.

Eichmann's trial began on April 11, 1961. It lasted several

1960年5月11日，侦探们布下了天罗地网。他们在埃克曼下班后跟踪他。当他沿着公路向前走时，一辆轿车经过他的身旁，突然停下。四个人跳了出来。埃克曼看到了他们开始尖叫。但是一名特工击中他的头部，然后把失去知觉的埃克曼扔到车子的后座上，便把车子开走了。最后特工们给以色列发出了暗语："野兽已经套上了锁链。"

特工们把埃克曼抓到了距离布宜诺斯艾利斯几英里远的一处隐蔽处。埃克曼以为他们要在那里杀掉他。"别杀我！"他乞求着，"请别杀我！"但是特工们根本就没想杀掉他。5月19日，他们把埃克曼装上一架包机，起飞前往以色列。

埃克曼的审讯在1961年4月11日正式开始。持续了几个月。在整个审

---

unconscious *adj.* 无意识的
intention *n.* 意图

hideout *n.* 隐匿处
chartered *adj.* 包租的；特许的

months. During the trial, Eichmann was kept in a *bulletproof* glass cage in the *courtroom*. The Israelis put him there to keep him alive. They didn't want anyone to shoot him before the trial was over.

Hundreds of witnesses were called. Many were Jews who had survived Eichmann's death camps. Still, Eichmann maintained he was not guilty. He argued that he had not personally killed anyone. He had simply arranged to send Jews to the camps. It was not his fault, he said, that they had been killed there. Besides, he protested, he was simply following orders. Wasn't that what good soldiers were supposed to do?

No one accepted these excuses. The whole world knew what Adolf Eichmann had done. On December 15, 1961, the court announced its *verdict*. Eichmann, his face pale and *twitchy*, rose to hear the words of Judge Moshe Landau: "The court finds you guilty."

讯期间，埃克曼被关在法庭的一个防弹玻璃笼子里面。以色列人把他关在那里是为了让他活着。他们不希望在审讯结束之前有人击毙他。

成百上千的目击证人被传唤了。他们中的许多人是在埃克曼的死亡集中营中幸存下来的。但是，埃克曼坚持他没有罪。他争辩说，他没有亲手杀死任何人，只是安排把犹太人送进了集中营。他说，他们在那里被杀掉不是他的错误。而且，抗议说，他只是在遵守命令。那不是好的士兵应该做的吗？

没有人接受这些托词。整个世界都知道阿道夫·埃克曼的所作所为。1961年12月15日，法庭宣布了对他的判决。埃克曼面色苍白，紧张不安，站起来听到莫什·兰多法官的话："法庭宣判你有罪。"

---

bulletproof *adj.* 防弹的　　　　　courtroom *n.* 法庭
verdict *n.* 裁定；判决　　　　　twitchy *adj.* 紧张不安的；担忧的

The court convicted Eichmann of war crimes. It also found him guilty of crimes against *humanity* and crimes against the Jewish people. The judges *rejected* Eichmann's claim that he was just following orders. As Judge Landau said, Eichmann was not "a *puppet* in the hands of others. He was among those who pulled the strings. This block of ice ... this block of marble ... closed his ears to the voice of his conscience."

Judge Landau asked Eichmann if he had anything to say. In Eichmann's final *statement*, he said, "I am not the monster I am made out to be."

The court—and the world—disagreed. Judges sentenced Adolf Eichmann to be hanged. The sentence was carried out on May 31, 1962. The man who had once claimed to be the "World's Number One Jew Killer" had finally been brought to justice.

　　法庭判处埃克曼战争罪。还判处他反人类罪和反犹太人民罪。法官驳回了埃克曼声称他是在遵守命令的说法。正如法官兰多所说，埃克曼不是"别人手中的傀儡。他属于那些用细绳拉着傀儡的人。这块坚冰……这块顽石……完全对他良知的声音充耳不闻。"

　　兰多法官问埃克曼还有没有什么要说的。在埃克曼的最终陈述中，他说："我不是那个被捏造出来的恶魔。"

　　法庭——和整个世界——不同意。法官宣判阿道夫·埃克曼处以绞刑。在1962年5月31日判决执行。这个声称是"世界上第一号犹太人杀手"的人终于伏法。

---

humanity *n.* 人类
puppet *n.* 傀儡

reject *v.* 拒绝；驳回
statement *n.* 陈述；说明

16

The Mad Bomber

Percy Wood was at his home in Lake Forest, Illinois, when an odd *package* arrived in the mail. *According to* the return address, it came from someone named "Enoch Fisher". Wood, who was the *president* of United Airlines, did not know anyone by that name. But several days earlier he had

This cabin in Montana was the workshop in which the "Unabomber," former mathematics professor Ted Kaczynski, assembled package bombs. Kaczynski eluded authorities for years while he sent and personally delivered his deadly mail.

疯狂的炸弹袭击者

这个位于蒙大拿州的小屋是"大学爆破者"、前数学教授泰得·卡辛斯基组装邮包炸弹用的。卡辛斯基多年以来一直在逃避着警方,并亲自发送他的致命信件。

帕西·伍德在位于伊利诺伊州雷克森林的家中,一封奇怪的信件送来了。按照回信地址,它是从一个叫作"爱诺克·菲什尔"的人发出的。伍德是联合航空公司的董事长,并不认识这个人。但是几天前他曾经收到一

---

package *n.* 包;包裹　　　　　　　　　　　　according to 根据;按照
president *n.* 主席;总裁

received a letter with the same return address. The letter had said Wood was about to get an interesting book in the mail. Since this new package was the size and shape of a book, Wood figured that's what it was. As he opened the package on June 10, 1980, however, it *exploded* in his hands. The bomb burned not only his hands but his face and a leg as well.

It turned out that there was no "Enoch Fisher". The return address led to a *deserted* lot in Chicago. As *authorities* investigated the case, they realized the attack was not an *isolated* act. Rather, it was the work of a serial bomber. Three other bombs had been planted in the Chicago area in the last two years. All bore certain markings that made experts sure they were the work of the same person. But who would do such a thing? And why?

个同样回信地址的人写的信。信中说伍德将收到一本很有趣的书。因为新来信件的形状、大小都与书相似，伍德想大概这个就是了。当时是1980年6月10日，他打开了信封，信在他的手中爆炸了。炸弹不仅烧伤了他的双手，而且他的脸和腿也受了伤。

后来证明根本就没有"爱诺克·菲什尔"这个人。回信地址是芝加哥的一个废弃的停车场。随着官方对这件事的调查，他们发现这次袭击不是一个孤立的行动，而是一个系列炸弹袭击者的行动。在过去的两年里，三枚炸弹被投放到了芝加哥地区。它们的标记相同，使专家们相信这是一个人所为。但是谁干的呢？为什么呢？

---

explode *v.* 爆炸
authority *n.* 官方；当局

deserted *adj.* 荒废的；废弃的
isolated *adj.* 孤立的；个别的

Police tried hard to figure out the *pattern* of the bombings. In each *instance* the targets had been people linked to universities or airlines. In addition, the bombs all seemed to come from Chicago. *Beyond* that, there was not much to go on. There was nothing else that tied the victims together.

Over the next few years three more bombings took place. Again, the targets were people connected with universities. But these bombs exploded in Utah, Tennessee, and California. Was the bomber on the move? What was motivating him? And who would be next?

By 1985 police had come up with a nickname for the bomber. They called him the "Unabomber" because he seemed so *obsessed* with universities. But they were really no closer to catching him—or

---

警方尽力来找出炸弹的规律。每一次，目标总是和大学或航空公司有关。而且，所有的炸弹好像都来自于芝加哥。除了这些，就没有什么有用的信息了。没有什么东西可以把受害者联系起来。

在后来的几年里，又有几个炸弹事件发生了，还是与大学有关的人。但是炸弹爆炸的地点是犹他州、田纳西州和加利福尼亚州。这个炸弹制造者是在变换位置吗？是什么在驱动着他？谁将是下一个？

1985年，警方给炸弹制造者起了个外号，叫他"大学爆破者"，因为他看起来是被大学迷住了。但是实际上他们没有接近他，或者她。从来没有人发现这个"大学爆破者"安置炸弹。

---

pattern *n.* 方式；形式
beyond *prep.* 除……外

instance *n.* 事例；实例
obsessed *adj.* 着迷的

her. The Unabomber had never been seen planting any of the devices.

Police believed the Unabomber was getting better at building bombs. They were right. On December 11, 1985, a man named Hugh Scrutton lost his life to a "Unabomb." As Scrutton stepped out of his California computer store, he saw a block of wood on the ground. He bent down and picked it up. When he did so, it blew up. Shrapnel flew in all directions. Much of the sharp metal *pierced* Scrutton's chest. Some *lodged* in his heart, killing him.

The Unabomber's next attack came in 1987. A computer repairman saw a *canvas* bag lying in the parking lot behind his shop in Salt Lake City, Utah. When he picked it up, the bag exploded. Again, *shrapnel* went flying. But this time the victim was lucky. He

---

　　警方认为"大学爆破者"的炸弹制造工艺得到了提高。他们是正确的。1985年12月11日一个叫作休·斯克拉顿的人被"大学爆破者"夺去了生命。当斯克拉顿走出他在加利福尼亚的电脑商店时，看到地上有一块木头。他弯下腰去拾起它。当他这样做时，木头爆炸了。里面的弹片飞向各个方向。许多这种尖利的金属片刺入了斯克拉顿的胸膛。有一些进入了他的心脏，要了他的命。

　　"大学爆破者"的下一次袭击发生在1987年。一个修理计算机的人在犹他州盐湖城自己商店后面的停车场上看到一个帆布袋。当他把它拾起来时，爆炸发生了。这一次，还是金属片飞了出来。但是这次受害者很幸

---

pierce v. 刺穿；透入
canvas n. 帆布

lodge v. 卡住；嵌入
shrapnel n. 弹片；碎片

was injured, but not killed.

There was another bit of luck involved with this attack. This time someone got a *glimpse* of the Unabomber. A woman happened to be looking out a window just a few yards from the parking lot. She saw a man place the canvas bag on the ground. He was a white man, about 5 feet 10 inches tall, with *reddish* hair and a *mustache*. She couldn't see much more than that because he was wearing a hooded sweatshirt and dark sunglasses. But at least it was something. At last the police had some clue as to what the Unabomber looked like.

By this time experts had also come up with a *psychological* profile of the killer. They believed he was intelligent and well educated. They thought he might once have held a teaching job. Perhaps he had

---

运。他只是受伤，没有丧命。

　　在这次袭击中，还是有点运气的。这次有人看到了大学爆破者。一位妇女偶然地从停车场几码远的地方向外看。他看到一个男人在地上放置了帆布袋。他是一个白人，大约5英尺10英寸高，长着红色的头发，留着小胡子。她无法看到更多的东西，因为他穿着一件带套头的运动衫，戴着深色的太阳镜。但至少，这也算是一些情况。最后，警方对于"大学爆破者"的模样有了一些线索。

　　此时，专家们对凶手的心理特征也有了了解。他们认为他很聪明，而且受过良好的教育。他们认为他有可能曾经做过教师的职业，可能被开除

---

glimpse *n.* 一瞥；一看

mustache *n.* 胡子

reddish *adj.* 微红的

psychological *adj.* 心理的

been fired. Or perhaps his job had been taken over by a computer. That would explain his anger toward universities and those in the computer field. Police questioned more than 200 *suspects* who fit the profile. But none *turned out* to be the Unabomber.

For the next six years the Unabomber was silent. Some people hoped he had been scared off for good. But on June 22, 1993, he showed that he was still out there, as dangerous and heartless as ever. On that day a *professor* at Yale University got a package in the mail. It was a bomb. Two days later the same thing happened to a professor in San Francisco. Both men were badly injured in the explosions.

By 1995 the Unabomber had sent out two more bombs. Both proved deadly. One killed a New Jersey *businessman*. The other killed

---

了。也可能是计算机取代了他的工作。这可以解释他对于大学和计算机领域的愤怒。警方讯问了200名符合此特征的嫌疑人。但是没有人符合这个"大学爆破者"。

以后的6年，"大学爆破者"陷入寂静。一些人希望他被吓退了，去做正常的工作了。但是1993年6月22日，他又一次出现了，还是那么危险，那么冷酷。那一天，耶鲁大学的一个教授收到一个邮件，是个炸弹。两天后，旧金山的一名教授发生了同样的事情。两个人都在爆炸中受重伤。

到1995年前，"大学爆破者"又发出了两枚炸弹。两起爆炸都使受害者丧生。一个杀害了一名新泽西的商人。另一个杀害了一名木材工业的演说员。

---

suspect *n.* 嫌疑犯
professor *n.* 教授

turn out 证明是；原来是
businessman *n.* 商人

a man who was a *lobbyist* for the timber industry.

By this time, there was a $1 million reward for information leading to the Unabomber's arrest and *conviction*. Police had set up a *hotline* to gather fresh leads. They also kept combing through past attacks, searching for clues. They noted, for instance, that all the bombings had been related to wood in some way. Some bombs had been encased in wood. Others had been sent to people named Wood or people living on streets with names connected to wood. But what exactly did that *signify*? Frustratingly, no one knew.

Meanwhile, people across the country worried about where the Unabomber might strike next. No one could feel safe with him on the loose. In September 1995 the Unabomber showed just how remorseless he was. On that day he sent a long letter to the *New*

　　到此时，为"大学爆破者"逮捕和判刑提供有用信息的悬赏额已经达到100万美元。警方设立了热线来搜集新的线索。他们还仔细梳理以前的袭击，寻找线索。比如他们还注意到，所有的爆炸都以某种形式与木材相关。一些炸弹被装在木头里面，还有一些邮寄给了叫作伍德的人，或者是居住的街道的名称与木头相关的人们。但是这又说明什么呢？令人困惑，没人知道。

　　当时，全国的人都害怕，这个"大学爆破者"的下一个袭击目标是谁呢？他逍遥法外，没有人能感觉到安全。1995年9月，"大学爆破者"展示了他是多么冷酷，不知悔改。那一天他给纽约《时代周刊》和《华盛顿

---

lobbyist *n.* 说客；专门受雇进行游说的人　　conviction *n.* 证明有罪；定罪
hotline *n.* 热线；专线电话　　signify *v.* 意味着；代表

York Times and the *Washington Post*. In it he said that he had sent the bombs to show his *hatred* for society. His goal, he said, was to destroy "the worldwide industrial system." He hoped his bombings would *encourage* people to *rise up* and *reject* modern technology. He didn't care that he had ruined people's lives. In his twisted mind, that was not important.

Many people were troubled by the Unabomber's words. But a man named David Kaczynski was downright shocked. David worked at a homeless shelter in New York state. He was a peaceful man who led a quiet life. "After I read the first few pages," David said, "my jaw literally dropped." He recognized many of the phrases that the Unabomber used. They were the same phrases his brother Ted had used in letters to him.

邮报》写信。其中他写道，他邮寄炸弹的目的是展示他对社会的仇恨。他的目标是去彻底毁灭"全世界的工业体系，"并希望他的爆炸行为能够鼓励人们起义，抵抗现代技术。他对夺走人的生命毫不关心。在他扭曲的思维中，那是不重要的。

许多人被"大学爆破者"的话吓坏了。但是，一个叫作大卫·卡辛斯基的人完全震惊了。大卫在纽约州的一个无家可归的人的避难所工作。他是一个过着平静生活的平和的人。"我读了最开始的几页后，"大卫说，"我着实吓了一跳。"他认出"大学爆破者"信中的许多短语的用法。这些用法与他兄弟泰得给他写信时的用法一模一样。

---

hatred *n.* 憎恨；仇恨
rise up 起义；反抗

encourage *v.* 鼓励；怂恿
reject *v.* 拒绝；抵制

David was not close to his brother. Theodore "Ted" Kaczynski lived alone in a small cabin in Montana. The two brothers had not seen each other in years. But David loved Ted. He was horrified to think Ted might be the Unabomber. Still, David knew he had to act. The lives of *innocent* people were at stake. In early 1996 David contacted the FBI and told them his *suspicions*.

A few weeks later, on April 3, Ted Kaczynski was arrested at his cabin. There the police found proof that he was indeed the Unabomber. They found *journals describing* his crimes. They also found parts of new bombs. Kaczynski pleaded guilty to the crimes and was sentenced to life in prison.

As it turned out, the police profile of the Unabomber had been right in many ways. He was a white man who had grown up in

---

大卫的居住地与他的兄弟的相距很远。西奥多·"泰得"·卡辛斯基居住在蒙大拿州的小木屋里。兄弟两人已经多年没有见面了。但是大卫热爱着他的兄弟。他被泰得，就是"大学爆破者"的想法给吓住了。但是大卫知道他应当行动。无辜百姓的生命存在着危险。1996年初，大卫联系了联邦调查局告诉了他们他的怀疑。

几个星期后，4月3日，泰得·卡辛斯基在他的木屋被逮捕。在那里警察发现他的确就是"大学爆破者"。他们找到了描写他罪行的杂志，还发现了新炸弹的部件。卡辛斯基对他的罪行供认不讳，被判处终身监禁。

最后我们来看看结果，警方对"大学爆破者"的描述在许多方面都是正确的。他是一个在芝加哥长大的白人。他聪明而且受过良好的教育。实

---

innocent *adj.* 无辜的
journal *n.* 报纸；杂志

suspicion *n.* 怀疑
describe *v.* 描述

Chicago. He was bright and well educated. In fact, he had gone to Harvard University. For a while Kaczynski had been an *assistant* professor of *mathematics*. But then he dropped out of *mainstream* life and *retreated* to the mountains of Montana. There he gardened, rode his bike, and worked with wood. No one could be sure what led Ted Kaczynski to commit his evil crimes. But everyone agreed that the world was a better place with him safely behind bars.

际上他在哈佛大学念过书。曾经有一段时间，卡辛斯基是数学助理教授。但是后来他离开了生活的主流，退隐到了蒙大拿的山区。在那里他种植一个小园子，骑自行车，和木头打交道。没有人确切地知道是什么导致卡辛斯基犯下如此邪恶的罪行。但是所有人都同意，他被捕入狱，世界美好多了。

---

assistant *adj.* 助理的
mainstream *n.* 主流

mathematics *n.* 数学
retreat *v.* 隐退；退却

17

"I Buried Paul"

The rain was coming down in sheets. The roads near London, England, were *slick* that early morning in 1966. Paul McCartney might have been driving too fast. Or perhaps he just didn't see a *curve* in the road. In any case, the singer lost control of his car. He crashed into a pole and died

The Beatles were the hottest music act in the world during the 1960s and early 1970s. How could the death of one of them be kept a secret? Many fans believed the Abbey Road album cover revealed evidence of Paul McCartney's death.

"我埋葬了保罗"

19世纪60年代和70年代早期，甲壳虫乐队是世界上最炙手可热的乐队。为什么其中一个成员的死亡却成了秘密？许多乐迷相信唱片《艾比路》的封面揭示出了保·麦卡特尼死亡的证据。

雨点轻轻落下。1966年的一个清晨，在英格兰，伦敦附近，路面非常湿滑。保罗·麦卡特尼可能是开车的速度太快。也许，他仅仅是没有注意到道路的一个拐弯。不管怎么说，这名歌手的小汽车失控了。他撞上一个栏杆，车辆燃烧起来，然后他就被烧死在里面。

slick *adj.* 光滑的   curve *n.* 弯曲；拐弯处

amid the flaming *wreckage*.

This was the *grim* story that spread in late 1969. At first, no one believed it. Paul McCartney could not be dead. No accident report had ever been filed. No death certificate had ever been issued. Besides, Paul was a member of the Beatles, the most famous rock group in the world. Fans saw him in concerts all the time. So of course he wasn't dead.

Or was he? According to the rumors, Paul had indeed died on a rainy road near London. His death had been kept a secret for three long years. The Beatles had covered up his fate because they didn't want their fans to know the truth. They feared it would hurt their popularity. And so, the story went, they hired a *fake* Paul to take the

---

　　这就是1969年末流传的那个残酷的故事。起初，根本没有人相信它。保罗·麦卡特尼不会死。根本没有事故报告，也没有签发出来的死亡证明。另外，保罗是甲壳虫乐队——世界上最著名的摇滚乐队的成员。乐迷们每时每刻都能在音乐会中见到他。那么，当然，他没有死。

　　难道他就是这么死的？据传，保罗其实是死于伦敦附近一条下着雨的路上。在长达三年的时间里，他的死因都是一个秘密。甲壳虫乐队没有说明他究竟怎样了，因为他们不想让乐迷知道真相，担心那样会影响他们的声望。因此，有消息说，他们雇来了一个假保罗来代替真的那个保罗的

---

amid *prep.* 在其中　　　　　　　wreckage *n.* （车辆或建筑物遭损毁后的）残骸
grim *adj.* 令人不快的；令人沮丧的　　fake *adj.* 假的

place of the real one. This second Paul looked, acted, and sang like the real thing. He played the guitar the same way and wrote the same kinds of songs. He was so good that he fooled everyone.

It is not clear how the *rumors* of Paul's death started. They might have begun with a Michigan student named Fred LaBour. He wrote an article for his college paper. In it, LaBour reviewed *Abbey Road*. This was the Beatles' latest album. LaBour claimed the album contained many clues that the real Paul was dead.

The rumors might have started at a radio station in Detroit. Three disc *jockeys* there were sure that Paul was dead. They passed their thoughts on to their listeners. Or perhaps the rumors came from a New York disc jockey named Roby Young. He, too, went on the air

---

位置。这第二个保罗在外貌、行为方式和演唱上都和真的那个一样。他吉他弹得和真保罗一样，并且能写出与真保罗同样风格的歌曲。他是如此出色，以至于愚弄了每一个人。

不清楚保罗已死的流言是如何产生的。那些流言可能是从一位名叫佛瑞德·拉波尔的密歇根的学生那里传出来的。他写了一篇大学论文。其中，他评价到了《艾比路》，这是甲壳虫乐队最后一张唱片。拉波尔说这张唱片当中包含很多真保罗已经死亡的线索。

那些流言可能是从底特律的一家无线电台开始传播的。那里的三名唱片灌制师确信保罗已经死了。他们把这些想法传递给了听众。也许这些流言来自纽约的一位唱片灌制师罗比·杨，他也凭空说到保罗已经死了。

---

rumor *n.* 谣言；传闻　　　　　　jockey *n.* 操作工

to say that Paul was dead.

It did not really matter how the rumors started. Once they began, they spread like wildfire. They were all that music fans could talk about for weeks. One radio station got more than 35,000 phone calls about Paul's death. Hundreds of *mourners* lined up in front of Paul's home in London. "The *panic* was *unquenchable*," said one writer.

So what was the "proof"? What convinced all these fans that Paul was dead? According to some people, clues were everywhere. All you had to do was look and listen. One piece of "evidence" was the *Abbey Road* album cover. It showed the four Beatles walking across a street called Abbey Road. That seemed normal enough. But a closer look *revealed* that Paul was out of step with the other three. He

---

流言究竟是从哪里产生的无关紧要。但流言一经传出，就如野火般四散开来，成为乐迷们成天谈论的话题。一家电台接到了超过35,000个询问保罗死讯的电话。许多悼念者在伦敦保罗的住宅前排起了长队。一位作家说："这种惊恐是无可置疑的。"

那么保罗死亡的"证据"是什么呢？什么才能让所有乐迷相信保罗确实死了呢？据有些人说，保罗已死的线索到处都是。你只需看一看，听一听就知道了。一条证据是唱片《艾比路》的封面，上面显示四位甲壳虫乐队成员正在穿过一条名为艾比路的街道。这张图片似乎十分正常，但是如果仔细观察，就会发现保罗与其他三位成员步调不一致。他是唯一赤脚行

---

mourner *n.* 哀悼者；送葬者
unquenchable *adj.* 无可非议的；无可置疑的

panic *n.* 恐慌；惊慌失措
reveal *v.* 显示；揭露

was the only one walking barefoot. And he was holding a cigarette in the wrong hand. These things were seen as important messages. They were considered hints from the Beatles about the awful truth: Paul really was dead.

One fan made a truly wild claim. When Vaseline was *smeared* on the cover of *Abbey Road*, the fan said, the face of Paul just faded away. That claim seemed pretty *far-fetched*. Still, the album cover *spooked* many Beatles fans.

Then there was the photo on the cover of the album *Sgt. Pepper's Lonely Hearts Club Band*. It pictured Paul wearing an O.P.D. patch. Frightened fans knew the meaning of those *initials*. They stood for an English police term. It meant "Officially Pronounced Dead." Hmmm ...

走的，并且把香烟拿在不恰当的那只手中。这些情况被当成重要的信号，它们被作为甲壳虫乐队传出的暗示，表达了一个极度糟糕的真相：保罗确实是死了。

一位乐迷提出了一个确实非常大胆的说法。这位乐迷说，只要把凡士林涂在《艾比路》的封面上，保罗的脸就会逐渐消失。这种说法似乎是不太容易被相信的。但是，这张唱片的封面确实引起了许多甲壳虫乐队的乐迷的紧张。

接着，有人发现唱片《佩珀中士的孤心乐队》封面上的照片也有问题。在这张图片上，保罗的衣服上的一个地方标有"O.P.D."字样。惊恐的乐迷们明白那些缩写的意思。它们代表着一个英国警察的术语，意思是"正式宣布死亡"。那么……

---

smear　*v.*　涂；抹　　　　　　　　far-fetched　*adj.*　牵强的
spook　*v.*　惊吓；吓唬　　　　　　initial　*n.*　（全名的）首字母

The most powerful clues came from the music itself. Fans became convinced that the Beatles' songs contained answers. They began to play the music faster or slower than usual. They taped many songs and then played them backward. By doing all this, they came up with several *startling* messages. One was John Lennon saying, "Paul is dead. Miss him. Miss him. Miss him."

One song that was played backward was "Revolution No. 9." Heard in *reverse*, the song seemed to contain the sounds of a car crash. People thought they heard flames *crackle*. And they heard a voice cry, "Get me out! Get me out!" Another voice seemed to say, "He hit a pole! We better get him to a *surgeon*." Then came a scream, followed by a voice saying, "My wings are broken." Finally, many

---

最有力的一个证据来自音乐本身。乐迷们开始相信甲壳虫乐队的歌曲本身包含着答案。他们开始比通常情况下或急或缓地放起了音乐。他们录下了很多歌曲，然后将其倒着播放出来。这样，他们得出几条令人吃惊的信息。其中之一是，约翰·列侬说："保罗死了。我们很怀念他，怀念他，怀念他。"

被倒着播放的歌曲中，有一首名叫"革命之九"。倒过来听时，这首歌似乎含有汽车撞击的声音。乐迷认为他们听到的就是车辆燃烧的噼啪声。他们还听到尖叫声："让我出去！我要出去！"另一个声音似乎在说："他撞到栏杆上了！我们最好赶快把他送到外科医生那里。"然后传来一声尖叫，接着有人说："我的胳膊断了。"最后，很多人听到了可怕

---

startling *adj.* 令人吃惊的
crackle *v.* 发出爆裂声

reverse *n.* 倒退；相反
surgeon *n.* 外科医生

people heard these *eerie* words: "Turn me on, dead man."

The song "Strawberry Fields" also created a *stir*. At the very end of the song, John Lennon spoke a few *garbled* words. His voice was low and slow. It was hard to tell what he was saying. But after playing it again and again, most people thought they had it figured out. Lennon was saying, "I buried Paul."

"Strawberry Fields" also contained the sound of a seagull. When speeded up, however, it sounded more like a man laughing. Was that Paul's voice? Was he laughing from the grave? It was a *chilling* thought.

As the clues piled up, more and more fans believed that Paul was dead. The Beatles, meanwhile, refused to comment on the rumors.

的话语："看着我呀，你这个死鬼！"

歌曲"草莓园"也引发了一场轰动。就在这首歌的最后，约翰·列侬说了一些含混不清的词语。他的声音低沉而又缓慢。很难分辨出他正在说的是什么。但是反复听过很多遍之后，大多数人认为他们听出来了他所说的话。列侬正在说："我埋葬了保罗。"

"草莓园"里还含有一些海鸥的声音。但是如果加快播放速度，那种声音听起来更像是一位男子正在大笑。那是保罗的声音吗？他正在坟墓里大笑？这真是一种令人胆战心惊的想法。

把这些线索联系在一起之后，越来越多的乐迷相信保罗确实死了。此时，甲壳虫乐队拒绝评论这些传言。有人认为这就证明了传言是真实的。

---

eerie *adj.* 可怕的；神秘的
garbled *adj.* 混乱的；含混不清的

stir *n.* 轰动；愤怒
chilling *adj.* 使人恐惧的；令人担心的

Some people thought that proved the rumors were true. Others said the Beatles' silence was just a publicity move. After all, the rumors didn't exactly hurt record sales. In fact, sales during this time *soared*. Fans *flocked* to buy Beatles albums. They wanted to hear any hidden messages the records might contain.

In late 1969 the Beatles spoke up at last. Paul McCartney was not dead, their agent said. In fact, the agent called the rumors "a load of old rubbish." Some fans refused to believe him. They didn't change their minds when shown recent pictures of Paul. They simply thought the pictures showed the fake Paul. "They won't take 'no' for an answer when told that Paul's alive," *grumbled* the agent.

Finally, the real Paul McCartney spoke out. "I am alive and well,"

还有人说甲壳虫乐队的沉默就是一种公开的表态。然而，这些传言并没有真正影响到唱片的销量。实际上，这一时期的销量急剧增加。乐迷们成群结队地购买甲壳虫乐队的唱片。他们想听出这些唱片中可能包含的任何一个隐藏的信息。

最终，1969年底，甲壳虫乐队开口说话了。保罗·麦卡特尼的代理人说，他没有死。实际上，这位代理人称这些传言是"一堆陈旧的垃圾"。有些乐迷拒绝相信他说的话。当看到保罗的近照之后，他们仍然没有改变看法。他们干脆认为照片上的是假保罗。这位代理人抱怨说："告诉他们保罗还活着的时候，他们连一声'不'都懒得说。"

最后，真保罗发言了。他说："我还活着，我很好。"这一下似乎

---

soar *v.* 急升；猛增　　　　　　　　flock *v.* 聚集；成群而行
grumble *v.* 发牢骚

he said. That seemed to satisfy most fans. A few continued to believe he was dead. But most accepted the truth. They were *relieved* that their *idol* had not died. But questions remained. Why all the "messages" in Beatles songs and albums?

As it turned out, most were not messages at all. There was no special meaning to the *Abbey Road* cover or the *Sgt. Pepper* photo. And there were no messages in songs played backward or at different speeds. People had just let their imaginations run wild. John Lennon did say something at the end of the song "Strawberry Fields." But he didn't say "I buried Paul." All he really said was "*cranberry sauce*."

说服了所有乐迷。还是有人坚持相信他死了，但是大多数人接受了这个事实。他们的偶像没有死，这使他们觉得获得了解脱。但还是有问题。甲壳虫乐队的歌曲和唱片里的所有那些"信息"是怎么回事？

事后证明，那些东西大多数都没有任何意义。《艾比路》的封面或者《佩珀中士》的照片没有什么特别含义。歌曲倒着或者以不同速度播放并没有包含什么特殊信息。人们只是想象的东西太多了。约翰·列侬在歌曲"草莓园"结尾确实说了一些话。但他说的不是"我埋葬了保罗"，实际上他说的只是"酸橘沙司"。

18

The Curse
of the Hope Diamond

Jean Baptiste Tavernier's eyes *lit up* when he saw it. An expert on rare *gems*, he *stared at* the diamond. It was huge. It was bigger than any diamond he had ever seen before. Its color was "a beautiful violet". There was just one problem. The diamond was *embedded in* a statue of the Hindu

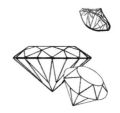

As diamonds go, the Hope diamond is not particularly large or costly. However, it has managed to gain quite a bad reputation among its previous owners.

钻石的诅咒

作为一颗钻石，希望钻石并不是特别巨大或者昂贵。然而，它却给以往的主人带去相当悲惨的命运。

看到它，吉恩·巴普迪斯特·塔沃尼眼前一亮。作为一位名贵珠宝的专家，他凝视着这颗钻石。这颗钻石大得惊人，比他以前曾经见过的任何一颗钻石都要大，呈"优美的蓝紫色"。唯一的问题是，这颗钻石被镶嵌在印度教神灵罗摩·悉多的雕像上。这颗闪闪发光的宝石装饰在这尊神像

---

light up 照亮；点亮
stare at 凝视；盯住

gem *n.* 宝石
embed in 嵌入

god Rama Sita. The glittering jewel decorated the god's forehead.

Tavernier approached the priests who watched over the statue. He asked if they would sell him the diamond. They said no. But Tavernier couldn't bear the thought of leaving India without it. So he ordered his men to *tie up* the priests. Then Tavernier *pried* the gem out of the statue and ran away.

No one is sure if this story is true. It is said to have taken place in 1642. But the life of Tavernier is *shrouded* in mystery. What we do know is that one way or another, Tavernier got his hands on the diamond.

We also know something else. For some strange reason, bad luck seemed to follow the diamond wherever it went. Was it *sheer*

的前额上。

　　塔沃尼走近看管这尊神像的僧侣，询问他们是否可以把这颗钻石卖给他。他们拒绝了他的要求。但是不拿到这颗钻石，塔沃尼根本就不想离开印度。所以塔沃尼命令部下缠住这些僧侣，然后他把这颗宝石从雕像上撬了下来，逃之夭夭。

　　没有人知道这个故事是否真实。据说这件事发生在1642年。但是塔沃尼的形迹从此神秘地被掩藏起来了。我们所知道的是，无论如何，塔沃尼确实得到了这颗钻石。

　　我们还知道另外一些事情。由于某种不为人知的原因，不论这颗钻石流落到何处，厄运似乎一直跟随着它。这纯粹是一种巧合吗？或者还有其

---

tie up 绑
shroud *v.* 覆盖

pry *v.* 撬开
sheer *adj.* 完全的；纯粹的

coincidence? Or was there more to it? Some people said that Rama Sita wanted *revenge* for the theft of the diamond. They said this god put a curse on the jewel.

Tavernier himself certainly came to an ugly end. In 1668 he sold the gem to King Louis XIV of France. After that he lost all his money. He moved to Russia. There he was attacked and killed by a pack of wild dogs. Louis XIV didn't do so well, either. He died a slow and painful death from *smallpox*. Was the "curse" of the stolen diamond to blame?

Back when Tavernier had the diamond, it was roughly cut and weighed $112 1/2$ *carats*. (Diamonds and other gems are measured in carats. A 112-carat gem is enormous. It would be about the size of a hen's egg.) Louis XIV had his jeweler cut the diamond into three

---

他原因？有人说罗摩·悉多想报复偷窃这颗钻石的行为。他们说这位神灵把诅咒放在了这颗宝石上。

塔沃尼自己的结局的确非常难堪。1668年，他把这颗宝石卖给法国国王路易十四，然后他倾家荡产了。他移居到了俄国。在那里，他遭到一群野狗攻击，然后死掉了。路易十四也未得善终。他得了天花，慢慢地，痛苦地死去了。这就是被偷的这颗钻石所施加的"诅咒"吗？

塔沃尼得到这颗钻石的时候，它已经被粗略切割过，重量是112.5克拉。（钻石和其他宝石是以克拉计量的。一颗112克拉的钻石是非常巨大的，大概会有鸡蛋大小。）路易十四和他的宝石匠把这颗钻石切割成3

---

coincidence *n.* 巧合
smallpox *n.* 天花

revenge *n.* 报复
carat *n.* 克拉

pieces. This gave each piece a greater *shine*. Reflecting light now made the pieces appear blue. The largest piece was cut in the shape of a heart. It weighed 67 carats and was called the French Blue. It was the most *dazzling* of the royal jewels.

In 1774 Louis XVI *inherited* this blue diamond. His wife, Marie Antoinette, wore it often. But in 1789 the "curse" struck again. The French people rose up in *revolt*. They turned against Louis and Marie. In 1793 they killed these two rulers by cutting off their heads.

The rebels put the blue diamond in a glass case for safekeeping. But it wasn't guarded very well. In 1792 someone walked off with it. The French Blue was never seen again.

Most experts believe it was taken to Spain and cut once again. Perhaps whoever had the French Blue knew that it was too famous

---

块。这种做法使其中每一块都展现出更美丽的光泽。现在，反射光使得这几块都呈现蓝色。最大的一块被切割成心形，重67克拉，被称为法国蓝钻石，是皇家宝石中最耀眼的一颗。

1774年，路易十六继承到这颗蓝钻石。他的妻子，玛丽·安托瓦内特经常戴着它。但是，1789年，"诅咒"再次袭来。法国人发动叛乱，反抗路易和玛丽。1793年，他们把这两个统治者送上了断头台。

叛乱者为了保护这颗蓝钻石，把它放在一个玻璃橱里。但是这颗钻石没有得到很好的守卫。1792年，有人把它带走了。从此再也没有人看见过法国蓝钻石。

多数专家相信，这颗钻石被带到西班牙，并且被再次分割。也许拿走法国蓝钻石的那个人知道，这颗钻石太出名了，不容易卖掉。不管怎么

---

shine *n.* 光泽；光彩

inherit *v.* 继承

dazzling *adj.* 耀眼的

revolt *n.* 叛乱；起义

to sell as it was. In any case, a piece of it *resurfaced* as an *oval* blue diamond. This one weighed 45^1/2 carats. In 1830 it came into the hands of a rich banker named Henry Philip Hope. From this point on, the stone was called the Hope Diamond.

Although the diamond had a new name, the old "curse" still seemed to be at work. Henry died without marrying. The diamond passed to his nephew's grandson, Sir Francis Hope. Francis married an American actress named May Yohe. So far, so good. But after a few years, May ran off with another man. Francis's life went from bad to worse. He went *bankrupt* and had to sell the diamond. Even so, he died in poverty. And the "curse" didn't spare May Yohe. She spent her last days *scrubbing* floors to make a living.

The next owner of the Hope diamond was a New York jeweler

说，法国蓝钻石的一部分重新露面了，这次是一块椭圆形的蓝钻石，重45.5克拉。1830年，这颗钻石落入一位名叫亨利·菲利普·霍普手中。因此，这颗宝石被叫作希望钻石。（"霍普"的英文"Hope"就是"希望"的意思。）

尽管这颗钻石有了一个新名字，但原来的"诅咒"似乎还在起作用。亨利至死没有结婚，钻石传给了他侄子的孙子弗朗西斯·霍普。弗朗西斯与一位名叫梅·约赫的美国女演员结婚。到目前为止，一切都还不错。但是几年后，梅跟着另一个男人跑了。弗朗西斯的生活状况越来越糟。他破产了，然后不得不卖掉这颗钻石。虽然如此，他还是在贫困潦倒中死去。并且"诅咒"也没有放过梅·约赫。在最后的岁月里，她是靠擦地板为生的。

希望钻石的下一位主人是一位名叫约瑟夫·弗兰克斯的纽约珠宝商。他

---

resurface *v.* 重新露面　　　　　　　　　oval *adj.* 椭圆的
bankrupt *adj.* 破产的；倒闭的　　　　　　scrub *v.* 擦洗

named Joseph Frankels. He, too, went broke. The diamond then passed from one person to the next. Simon Montharides, a Greek gem merchant, had it for a time. But he, his wife, and their children all died in a mountain accident. They fell off a *cliff*. For a while, the Sultan of Turkey, Abdul Hamid, owned the stone. But like Louis XVI, he was *overthrown* in a revolution.

A Russian prince named Kanitovski bought the diamond. He gave it to a French singer named Lorens Laduc. It was said that Kanitovski loved Laduc. But the day after giving her the diamond, he killed her. He himself was later *stabbed* to death.

Despite the "curse" of the Hope diamond, people still wanted to own it. In 1912 an American named Evalyn McLean bought the Hope diamond. She paid $154,000 for it.

的命运也很悲惨。然后这颗宝石从一个人手里传到另一个人手里。一位希腊珠宝商人西蒙·曼特雷德曾经得到过它。但是他本人，妻子，他们的孩子全都死于一次山难。他们摔到一个悬崖下面。土耳其苏丹阿卜杜勒·哈密德曾经得到过这块宝石。但是和路易十六一样，他在一次革命中被推翻了。

一位俄国王子卡尼托夫斯基买下了这块钻石，把它送给了一位法国歌手劳伦斯·拉杜克。据说卡尼托夫斯基爱上了拉杜克。但是把钻石给她的第二天，卡尼托夫斯基就把她杀了。而他自己后来被刺死。

尽管有着关于希望钻石的"诅咒"，人们还是想要拥有它。1912年，一位名叫艾芙琳·麦克林的美国人买下了希望钻石，这花费了她154,000美元。

---

cliff　*n.*　悬崖　　　　　　　　　　overthrow　*v.*　推翻；颠覆
stab　*v.*　刺；刺伤

McLean didn't believe in the "curse." To her, all the death and dying that surrounded the gem was just bad luck. McLean wore the Hope diamond almost all the time. When she didn't have it on, she *stuffed* it in a *cushion*. She hired a guard to keep it from being stolen.

Perhaps Evalyn McLean should have hired a second guard to watch over herself and her family. After all, some would say the "curse" had not yet run its course. McLean's son died in a car crash. Her daughter died from an *overdose* of sleeping pills. She and her husband nearly divorced. He spent his last days in a hospital for the *mental* illness .

Evalyn McLean herself died in 1947. With her death, the "curse" of the Hope diamond seems to have ended. Harry Winston bought the stone two years later. For about 10 years, he showed the Hope

---

　麦克林不相信"诅咒"的存在。对她来说，所有与这颗宝石有关的那些死亡和濒临死亡的人都只是运气不好罢了。麦克林几乎一直佩戴着希望钻石。不戴时，她就把这颗钻石放在一个衬垫上。她还雇了一名卫兵看守它，防止被盗。

　也许艾芙琳·麦克林应该再雇一名卫兵保护她自己和她的家人。毕竟，有人会说那个"诅咒"还没有结束。麦克林的儿子死于一次车祸，她的女儿因服用安眠药过量而死亡，她和丈夫几乎要离婚了。她丈夫因患有精神方面的疾病，在一家医院里度过了最后的岁月。

　艾芙琳·麦克林自己死于1947年。随着她的死亡，希望钻石的"诅咒"似乎结束了。两年后，哈里·温斯顿买下这块宝石。大约10年时间

---

stuff *v.* 填塞；塞满
overdose *n.* 使用过量

cushion *n.* 垫子
mental *adj.* 精神病的

diamond in *exhibits* around the world. Then, in 1958, he gave it to the Smithsonian Institution. Believe it or not, Winston sent this priceless gem through the mail. He spent just $2.44 on *postage*! Luckily, it arrived safely.

The Hope diamond has been on public *display* ever since it got to the Smithsonian. It is one of the top tourist sights in Washington, D.C. Each day, thousands of people line up to see it. No tragic pattern has been found among those who view the diamond. Does that mean Rama Sita's "curse" has finally been lifted? Or does evil still *lurk* within that beautiful blue stone?

里，他在世界各地的展览中都展示过希望钻石。然后，在1958年，他把这颗钻石送给史密森学会。不论你是否相信，温斯顿是通过邮件把这颗价值连城的宝石送出去的。他只花费了2.44美元的邮资！幸运的是，宝石安全地到达那里。

从到达史密森学会一直到现在，希望钻石都被公开陈列着。它是哥伦比亚特区华盛顿的顶级观光景点之一，每天都有几千人排队观看。在观看这颗钻石的人中间，并未见到有悲惨的事情发生。这意味着罗摩·悉多的"诅咒"最终消失了呢？或者，厄运还潜藏在那颗美丽的蓝宝石中吗？

exhibit *n.* 展览
display *n.* 展示

postage *n.* 邮资
lurk *v.* 潜藏；埋伏

19

Escape to Freedom

Frederick Douglass's mother died when he was just six years old. Douglass, who was a *slave*, *ended up* fending for himself. Every day he did the *chores* his masters required. At night he slept on the dirt floor of an old shack. He had no shoes, no coat, not even a *decent* pair of pants.

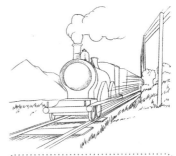

This train, pulled by a steam locomotive, is the type that carried Frederick Douglass to freedom.

自由大逃亡

这列蒸汽机车牵引的火车就是当年把弗里德洛克·道格拉斯带到自由之地的那种列车。

当弗里德洛克·道格拉斯6岁时，他的母亲死了。道格拉斯是个奴隶，他得自己保护自己。每天他都要做他主人要求的事情。晚上，他在一个破旧房间的地上睡觉。他没有鞋，没有衣服，甚至没有像样点的裤子。

slave *n.* 奴隶
chore *n.* 日常琐事

end up 结束；最终到达
decent *adj.* 像样的

He rarely got enough to eat. To fill his stomach, he sometimes took an egg from the barn or an ear of corn from the field. Other times he fought the dogs for *crumbs* from under the master's table.

In 1826, when he was eight years old, his Maryland owners sent him to the city of Baltimore. There he went to work for Hugh and Sophia Auld. The Aulds treated him kindly. They gave him food, clothes, and a warm bed to sleep in. Sophia Auld even began teaching him to read, but her husband soon put a stop to that. Once slaves learned to read, he *warned*, they would start getting ideas out of books. Then they would become unhappy with their lives as slaves. They might even *figure out* a way to get free.

Douglass heard what Hugh Auld said. He decided to keep working on his reading, no matter what. As the years passed,

他很少能够吃饱。为了填饱肚子，有时他从谷仓偷一个鸡蛋，或者从田地中偷一穗玉米。有时他还在主人的桌子底下与狗打架抢食物碎屑。

1826年，当时他8岁，他的马里兰州的主人把他送到巴尔的摩市。这里，他为休·奥德和索非亚·奥德工作。奥德一家对他很好。他们给他食物、衣服和舒服的床。索非亚·奥德甚至开始教他读书，但是很快她的丈夫阻止了她。他警告道，一旦奴隶学会了读书，他们就会从书籍中得到观点。那么他们就会不满奴隶的处境，甚至会想出逃跑的办法。

道格拉斯听到了休·奥德所说的话。他决定无论多难，都要继续读书学习。随着年龄的增长，道格拉斯发现了提高阅读技巧的方法。他阅读旧

crumb *n.* 食物碎屑
figure out 想出；明白

warn *v.* 警告

Douglass found ways to *improve* his reading skills. He read old papers. He read posters and signs. At the age of 12, he paid 50 cents to buy his first book. One of the stories in the book was about a slave who read so well and knew so much that he was able to talk his master into setting him free. That story gave Douglass even more incentive to become a good reader.

By 1838 Hugh Auld had died, and Frederick Douglass had been sent to work in a Baltimore shipyard. It was there that he put together a *bold* plan. He decided to make a run for *freedom. In order to* succeed, he would have to get out of Maryland. He would have to make it to one of the northern states, where slavery was illegal. Douglass knew that if he were caught he would be whipped and chained. He might even be killed. But he was willing to risk death for

---

报纸、海报和标志。当他12岁时，他花50美分买了他的第一本书。其中有一个故事就是关于一名奴隶。这名奴隶阅读非常好，懂得很多，甚至说得他的主人愿意把他释放了。这个故事给了道格拉斯一个要成为知识渊博的人的动机。

1838年，休·奥德去世，弗里德洛克·道格拉斯被送到巴尔的摩的一个造船厂工作。在那里他有了一个大胆的计划，决定为自由而逃跑。要想成功，他得逃出马里兰州，逃到北部的州，在那里奴隶制是非法的。道格拉斯知道，如果他被抓住，将被鞭笞或者锁住，甚至被杀。但是为了自由，他愿意冒死亡的危险。

---

improve *v.* 改善；增进
freedom *n.* 自由

bold *adj.* 大胆的；冒风险的
in order to 为了

the chance to be free.

Douglass already knew some blacks who were free. Known as "freemen," each of them carried "free papers". The *documents* proved that the holder was free and not a slave. Once in a while, a slave would borrow someone's "free papers" to make an escape. When the *runaway* reached a free state, he or she would send the papers back. The trick was to get the papers from someone who looked like you. The papers stated such things as height, weight, color of skin, any scars, and so forth.

Douglass did not know any freemen who looked much like him. He did, however, have a black friend who was a *sailor*. This man had a set of papers stating that he was a free American sailor. At the top of the page was an American *eagle*. It looked very impressive.

道格拉斯认识一些自由的黑人，他们叫作"自由人"，他们都有"自由证明"。它能证明携带者是自由人而不是奴隶。有时，一名奴隶可能借别人的"自由证明"来逃亡。当他/她逃到了自由的州，就会把证明送回来。诀窍是要找到一个长相与你相似的人。证明文件会写明一些特征，如：身高、体重、皮肤颜色、伤疤等等。

道格拉斯认识的自由人中没有长相与他相像的。但是，他有一个黑人朋友是一名水手。这个人有一整套的文件说明他是一名自由的美国水手。在证明页的上方是一只美国鹰，看起来很动人。道格拉斯想这些证明大概

---

document *n.* 文件；公文
sailor *n.* 水手；船员

runaway *n.* 逃走的人；逃亡者
eagle *n.* 鹰

Douglass thought that these papers might work like "free papers". Unfortunately, the papers called for someone with skin much darker than Douglass's. Still, Douglass decided it was worth a chance. He would use the sailor's papers to make a break for freedom.

From Maryland the nearest free state was Pennsylvania. The best way to get there was by train. But Douglass couldn't just walk into the train station and buy a ticket. His papers would be checked too closely. So he waited until the train was pulling out of the station. Only then did he *hop* on board. He *was dressed in* a borrowed sailor's suit. He tried to look calm, but every nerve inside his body was on edge.

After a while, the *conductor* began checking tickets. When he got to the car carrying blacks, he also checked their papers. The conductor

---

可以做"自由证明"来用。但是这些证明指明的肤色比道格拉斯要黑得多。但是道格拉斯认为值得一试。他想使用水手的证明来逃往自由之地。

　　距离马里兰州最近的自由州是宾夕法尼亚州。最好的方法就是坐火车到那里。但是道格拉斯不能直接走进火车站去买车票。他的证明文件会受到仔细地检查。所以他等待着，直到他要坐的火车出站了，他健步跳上了车。他身穿借来的水手服。他尽量地保持冷静，但是他身上的每一个神经细胞都是极度紧张。

　　过了一会，列车员开始检票。当到达黑人车厢时也检查证件，列车员

---

hop *v.* 跳跃　　　　　　　　　　　　be dressed in 穿……的服装
after a while 过了一会　　　　　　　　conductor *n.* 售票员

acted rude to some of the people in the car. This made Douglass even more nervous. But the conductor's face brightened when he got to Douglass. Perhaps it was because of the sailor's *uniform*. Most Americans had kind feelings for sailors at this time.

Still, the conductor had a job to do, so he said to Douglass, "I suppose you have your free papers?"

"No, sir," answered Douglass. "I never carry my free papers to sea with me."

"But you have something to show that you are a freeman, haven't you?"

"Yes, sir," said Douglass, "I have a paper with the American eagle on it."

Douglass *handed over* his papers to the conductor. The man

对车厢中的一些人很粗暴，这时道格拉斯更紧张。但是当列车员走到道格拉斯跟前时脸色缓和了下来，可能因为水手服的原因。当时大部分的美国人对水手很有好感。

列车员还是要完成工作，所以他对道格拉斯说："能看看你的自由文件吗？"

"没有，先生，"道格拉斯回答道，"我从来不带着自由证明文件出海。"

"但是你要有什么东西证明你是自由的，对吧？"

"是的，先生，"道格拉斯说，"我有一张带美国鹰的文件。"

道格拉斯把他的文件递给了列车员。那个人几乎没有看那个证件。

---

uniform *n.* 制服   hand over 交出

barely *glanced at* them. He took Douglass's ticket money and left. Douglass was thrilled, but he was not out of danger yet. He was still in Maryland. He might be discovered and arrested at any moment. "I saw on the train several persons who would have known me in any other clothes," wrote Douglass. Amazingly, the sailor's uniform seemed to fool them all.

Slowly, the train moved north. To Frederick Douglass the minutes seemed like hours. At one station Douglass looked out the window and caught his breath. Just a few feet away was a man named Captain McGowan. Douglass had done work for him earlier that week. If McGowan noticed him, Douglass's plan would be *foiled*. Luckily, McGowan didn't look Douglass's way.

"This was not my only hair-breadth escape," wrote Douglass.

他拿起道格拉斯的票款就离开了。道格拉斯很兴奋，但是他还没有脱离危险。他还在马里兰州的境内。在任何时候他都有可能被发现，被逮捕。"我发现在车上，如果我不是穿水手服，好几个人就会认出我来，"道格拉斯写到。奇怪的是看起来水手服好像把他们都骗住了。

火车缓慢地向北行进。对于弗里德洛克·道格拉斯来说，分钟就好像是小时一样漫长。在一个火车站，道格拉斯向窗外看，屏住了呼吸。几英尺远的地方站着一个人，叫作麦克高瓦上尉。道格拉斯在前几天曾经给他干过活。如果麦克高瓦注意到他，道格拉斯的计划就泡汤了。幸运的是，麦克高瓦没有向道格拉斯这边看。

"极度的危险不止这一次，"道格拉斯写道。一次，一个认识道格

---

glance at 看；浏览

foil *v.* 阻止；击退

At one point a German blacksmith who knew Douglass well looked straight at him. After a few seconds, he went back about his business. "I really believe he knew me," wrote Douglass, "but had no heart to *betray* me."

At last Douglass reached Philadelphia, Pennsylvania. Quietly but *joyfully,* he moved on to New York City. In less than 24 hours, he had gone from being a slave to being a free man. "No man now had a right to call me his slave," wrote Douglass.

Douglass kept the *details* of his escape a secret for more than 40 years. He didn't want to hurt other slaves who might use the same plan. Escaping was hard enough without giving away any secrets to slave owners. Also, Douglass didn't want to cause trouble for anyone who had helped him. Helping a slave to escape was a high crime. As

---

拉斯的德国铁匠与他的目光相对。过了几秒钟，他又继续干他的事情了。"我知道他认出我了，"道格拉斯写道，"但是他并不想出卖我。"

最后，道格拉斯到达了宾夕法尼亚的费城。他很平静，但很快乐。他又朝着纽约进发了。在24小时之内，他已经从奴隶转变成为自由人。"现在没有人有权力管我叫他的奴隶，"道格拉斯写道。

道格拉斯把他逃亡计划的细节当作秘密保留了40年。他不想伤害其他使用同样方法逃亡的奴隶。能够在奴隶主面前保守秘密逃跑已经是很不容易了。而且道格拉斯不想给那些帮助过他的人找麻烦，帮助奴隶逃亡是重罪。就如同道格拉斯所说，"就是谋杀也不会受到如此严厉的处罚。"

---

betray *v.* 出卖；背叛
detail *n.* 细节

joyfully *adv.* 高兴地

Douglass said, "Murder itself was not more sternly punished."

Frederick Douglass went on to become world famous. He spent years fighting slavery. He published his own newspaper, called The *North Star*. Douglass wrote best-selling books about his life. He made friends with white leaders such as Abraham Lincoln. He *urged* the president to free the slaves. In 1863 Lincoln freed all the slaves in the southern states. So Douglass, who died in 1895, lived to see his people freed.

Over the years Frederick Douglass was often asked now his first day of freedom felt. He said, "I felt as one might feel upon escape from a *den* of hungry lions." He added, "My chains were broken, and the *victory* brought me *unspeakable* joy."

弗里德洛克·道格拉斯继续为世界人民所熟知。他长时期与奴隶制做斗争,并出版了自己的报纸《北方之星》。道格拉斯写的关于他一生的书成了畅销书。他与白人领袖,如亚伯拉罕·林肯,交上了朋友。他要求总统释放奴隶。1863年林肯释放了所有南方各州的奴隶。这样在道格拉斯1895年去世之前终于看到了他的人民得到释放的一天。

多年以来,弗里德洛克·道格拉斯经常被问及他得到自由的第一天的感受。他说:"我的感觉就好像是从布满饥饿狮子的洞穴中逃出来一样,"他又补充道,"我的锁链被打破了,胜利给我带来了无法用语言来形容的愉快。"

---

urge *v.* 力劝;敦促

victory *n.* 胜利

den *n.* 兽穴

unspeakable *adj.* 无法形容的

Firebomb on the Subway

Denfield Otto was running late. The off-duty transit officer rushed onto the New York City *subway* on December 21, 1994. As he hopped on the sixth car of the Number 4 train headed to Brooklyn, he hoped he wouldn't be late for *choir* practice at St. Philip's Church. But Otto didn't make it to the church that day. A firebomb

The New York subway carries millions of people to their destinations every day. Unfortunately, the crowded subway cars have been the targets of violent attacks, such as Edward Leary's firebomb explosion.

地铁上的燃烧弹

纽约的地铁每天都要运送数以百万计的旅客。不幸的是，人群拥挤的地铁车厢成为暴力犯罪的目标，爱德华·里瑞的燃烧弹袭击就是个例子。

丹菲尔德·奥托走得很晚。这位刚刚下班的运输官员挤进了纽约的地铁，这一天是1994年12月21日。他跳上了开往布鲁克林的4号列车，第六节车厢，希望能够赶上圣菲利普教堂的唱诗班练习。但是奥托没有到达目的地。一枚燃烧弹打乱了他的计划。

subway *n.* 地铁   choir *n.* 唱诗班

interrupted his plans.

The Number 4 train was crowded with office workers and holiday shoppers laden with gifts. Most of these people were on their way somewhere. But one person on board had a different *agenda*. He was Edward Leary, a 49-year-old man from New Jersey. Leary wanted to kill or maim as many passengers as possible. It was all part of a twisted *scheme* he had to *extort* money from the transit system. Once he had killed some people, he planned to use the threat of more violence to collect big sums of money. A week earlier Leary had made a test run. He set off a firebomb in a different train. That fire badly burned two students.

Now Leary was on the Number 4. There was nothing unusual in the way he was dressed. He wore a hat, a dark blue coat, blue

---

4号列车中挤满了办公室的工作人员和假日的购物者，他们都带着礼物。绝大多数都在匆忙地赶往某处。但是他们中有一个人抱着不同的念头，他叫作爱德华·里瑞，49岁，来自新泽西州。里瑞打算尽可能多地杀伤乘客。这只是他邪恶计划的一部分：他要向运输系统敲诈钱财。他曾经杀死了一些人，打算用更血腥的暴力活动来获得大量的金钱。一个星期前，里瑞曾经做了一次试验。他在一辆列车上引爆了一枚燃烧弹使两名学生严重烧伤。

现在里瑞在4号列车上。他的穿着打扮完全没有什么特别，他戴着礼帽，身着深蓝色的上衣，蓝色牛仔裤，脚踏运动鞋，手里拿着一个纸袋。

---

interrupt *v.* 打断；打扰　　　　　agenda *n.* 日常工作事项；议程
scheme *n.* 计划；方案　　　　　　extort *v.* 敲诈；强夺

jeans, and sneakers. In his hands he carried a paper bag. *Witnesses* later told the police that they saw him *fumbling* with something inside the bag. Some people also noticed an odd smell, like gasoline. One woman moved away from Leary after seeing his bag and smelling the gasoline. But Denfield Otto, who was just 15 feet away, never noticed Leary.

Shortly after 1:30 P.M., the Number 4 pulled into Fulton Street Station. Everything seemed normal. But just as the train doors began to open, *commuters* heard a loud pop. To some it sounded like a cherry bomb. Then suddenly a ball of fire engulfed the train and its passengers. People's clothing and hair caught fire. Some started running around, wildly beating their clothes to kill the flames. Others rolled on the floor of the train or on the concrete *platform* in

---

目击者后来告诉警方，他的手在袋子里面曾经摸索着什么东西。也有人注意到了一种奇怪的气味，好像是汽油。有一名妇女在看到里瑞在袋子里摸索，并闻到汽油味道后远远地离开了他。但是在15英尺外的丹菲尔德·奥托一直没有注意到里瑞。

刚过下午1:30，4号列车驶进了凡尔顿大街车站。看起来好像一切正常。但是就在列车门打开时，乘客们听到了一声响亮的爆炸声。对一些人来说，好像是一个大爆竹爆炸的声音。突然一个大火球裹住了列车和乘客们，人们的衣服和头发着火了。有一些人开始四处乱跑，疯狂地拍打身上的火焰。另一些人在列车的地板上或月台上打滚，试图熄灭身上的火焰。

---

witness *n.* 目击者
commuter *n.* 通勤者；上下班往返的人
fumble *v.* 摸索；笨手笨脚地寻找某物
platform *n.* 月台；站台

an *attempt* to *snuff out* the fire.

"Everyone was on fire and they were screaming and hollering and running," recalled Alma Foster. "It was the scariest thing. I didn't think I was going to make it. I thought I was going to get trampled."

When Denfield Otto saw the blaze, he dashed out the door and ran for a token booth. There he grabbed a fire *extinguisher* and ran back to train. He aimed it at two people who were lying on the floor of the train in flames. He extinguished the fire on both of them, in all likelihood saving their lives.

Meanwhile James Nobles, a token clerk, instantly saw what was happening. He hit the emergency switch, bringing police and *medics* quickly to the rescue. Everyone started working together. As Denfield Otto said, "Black and white, it made no difference. One guy burning

---

"所有人都着了火，他们尖叫着、大喊着，四处乱跑，"艾尔玛·福斯特回忆道，"这真是可怕。我没有想到我还能活着，我以为我要被踩倒了。"

当丹菲尔德·奥托看到发生的大火，他冲出了门，冲向一个火警柜。他在那里抓起了一个灭火器跑回来。他对准两名倒在车厢地面上，身上起火的人，扑灭了他们身上的火，也可以说是救了他们的命。

当时詹姆斯·诺贝尔思是一名警卫，看到了这个突发情况。他打开警报，让警察和救护人员迅速赶到现场。所有的人开始共同工作。正如丹菲尔德·奥托所说："黑人、白人此时是没有分别的。一个浑身着火的人是

---

attempt *n.* 试图；努力
extinguisher *n.* 灭火器

snuff out 扑灭；熄灭
medic *n.* 医学工作者；医生

was a black guy, and white and black were beating out the flames."

New Yorkers hailed Otto as a hero. Mayor Rudolph Giuliani praised his "immediate and brave response." President Bill Clinton called to congratulate him. A reporter asked Otto how it felt to be a hero. He shrugged his shoulders and said that he didn't see himself as a hero. "I only did my job," he answered.

Despite his *modesty*, Otto was a hero. So were several others. Total strangers risked their lives to beat out the fires on people next to them. Mary McMurry was one such hero. She came to the aid of three fellow passengers. "They were burning, laying there burning," she said. "Whatever we could do, we rolled them on the ground and threw *jackets* on them [to squelch the flames]."

Curt Jackson was one of the burn victims. Still, that didn't stop

---

黑人，无论白人还是黑人大家一起把他身上的火扑灭。"

纽约人称奥托是个英雄。市长鲁道夫·尤拉尼赞扬了他的"迅速而勇敢的反应。"比尔·克林顿总统对他表示祝贺。一名记者问奥托作为一名英雄有什么感受。他耸了耸肩说他并没有自认为是个英雄。"我只是做了我的工作，"他是这样回答的。

尽管他很谦虚，奥托的确是个英雄。还有其他的几个人。完全是素不相识的人冒着生命危险把他们身边人身上的火扑灭。玛丽·麦克莫利就是这样的一个英雄。她冲上去帮助三名乘客。"他们身上起火了，躺在那里起火了，"她说，"我们想尽办法来帮助他们，我们推他们在地上滚，用上衣在他们的身上抽打[来扑灭火焰]。"

科特·杰克森是当时火灾的受害者之一。但这也没有阻止他去帮助别

---

modesty *n.* 谦逊

jacket *n.* 夹克；短上衣

him from helping others. "All I remember was a bang going off," he said later from his hospital bed. "[Then] I felt my face burning." He ran from the train in pain. But when Jackson saw another person burning on the platform, he stopped and put out the fire with his jacket.

Miraculously no one was killed. Still, 50 people were burned, four critically. Alina Badia, a medic, was one of many who *rushed to* the station. The scene there looked like a war zone. "We pulled up and it was like a *swarm* of people with burns," said Badia. "Their skin was *blackened* ... the burns were so deep they were bleeding from them. Their clothes were stuck to their bodies ... one man, when we cut his *gloves* off, his skin came with it."

One of the victims, it turned out, was Edward Leary himself. It

人。"我所记得的就是砰的一声，"后来他躺在医院的病床上说。"[然后]我感到我的脸在燃烧。"他十分疼痛，从车上冲了出去。但是当杰克森看到另一个人在月台上燃烧时，他停了下来用他的外衣帮助他扑灭身上的火。

称得上是奇迹的是没有人在这次事件中丧生。但还是有50个人被烧伤，4个人伤势严重。艾利娜·巴迪亚是一名急救人员，也是冲向现场的人员之一。当时的场景就好像是战场。"我们冲了上去，那是一大群满是烧伤的人，"巴蒂娜说，"他们的皮肤变黑……烧伤伤口很深，渗透着血。他们的衣服粘到了身体上……有一个人，当我们把他的手套剪下来时，他的皮也跟着粘下来了。"

最后发现，其中一名受害者是爱德华·里瑞自己。看起来他自酿的

rush to 火速赶往　　　　　　　　　swarm *n.* 一大群
blacken *v.* （使）变黑　　　　　　glove *n.* 手套

seemed that his *homemade* bomb had gone off before he intended. Badly burned, Leary escaped by hopping onto another subway train. He then *switched* to a second train. Finally the police spotted him a mile away in Brooklyn. At first they thought he was another victim. His *sneakers* and jeans were burned. So was two-thirds of his body. Some of the skin on his face was *peeling off*. The police quickly called an ambulance to rush him to the hospital.

En route to the hospital, ambulance workers heard a radio description of the suspect. He was white, about 200 pounds, between 40 and 50 years old, wearing blue jeans and a dark blue coat. A police officer who was riding in the ambulance looked back at Leary. "Wait a minute," he said to another officer. "That sounds like the guy that we have."

炸弹在它安排好之前爆炸了。里瑞也受了重伤，他跳上另一辆地铁列车逃跑。然后他又换了一次车。最后警方还是在一英里外的布鲁克林发现了他。最初，他们以为他也是一名受害者。他的鞋和牛仔裤都烧坏了，身体的三分之二也烧伤了，甚至脸上的一些皮肤也脱落下来。警方马上叫了一辆救护车把他送往医院。

在去往医院的路上，救护车的工作人员听到无线电广播中描述犯罪嫌疑人的情况。他是个白人，大约200磅重，40岁至50岁，穿着蓝色牛仔裤和深蓝色上衣。驾驶救护车的警官回过头看了看里瑞。"等等，"他对另一名警察说，"听起来好像是我们这里的这个家伙。"

---

homemade *adj.* 自制的
sneakers *n.* 运动鞋

switch *v.* 改变；转变
peel off 脱掉；剥落

Leary was quickly arrested. The police charged him with 45 counts of *attempted* murder. On May 2, 1995, a court found him guilty of the charges. Judge Rena Uviller sentenced him to 94 years in prison. That was the maximum sentence allowed by law. In her final statement, Judge Uviller said, "Evil exists in this world. There is no reason for it. It's just there. And we are looking at it in the person of Edward Leary."

There is also good in the world. We see that when we look at people *such as* Mary McMurry, Curt Jackson, Alina Badia, and Denfield Otto.

里瑞马上被逮捕。警方指控他45项蓄意谋杀。在1995年5月2日，法庭宣布罪名全部成立。法官里拿·尤维勒宣判他服刑94年，这是法律允许的最长刑期。在尤维勒法官的最终陈述中，她说："世界上存在着邪恶，毫无理由，就是存在着。这里我们在爱德华·里瑞的身上就能见到。"

世上也存在着友善。我们可以从如同玛丽·麦克莫利、科特·杰克森、艾利娜·巴迪亚和丹菲尔德·奥托身上见到。

---

attempted *adj.* 企图的；未遂的　　　　such as 比如